D0283867

LADY GAGA:

BEHIND THE FAME

LADY GAGA:
BEHIND THE FAME

EMILY HERBERT

THE OVERLOOK PRESS

NEW YORK

This edition first published in paperback in the United States and Canada in 2010 by

The Overlook Press, Peter Mayer Publishers, Inc.
141 Wooster Street
New York, NY 10012

Copyright © 2010 by Emily Herbert

All rights reserved. No part of this publication may be reproduced or transmitted in any form or by any means, electronic or mechanical, including photocopy, recording, or any information storage and retrieval system now known or to be invented, without permission in writing from the publisher, except by a reviewer who wishes to quote brief passages in connection with a review written for inclusion in a magazine, newspaper, or broadcast.

Internal photographs courtesy of Rex Features.

Cataloging-in-Publication Data is available from the Library of Congress

Book design and typeformatting by Bernard Schleifer
Manufactured in the United States of America
FIRST EDITION
2 4 6 8 10 9 7 5 3
ISBN 978-1-59020-423-8

CONTENTS

LADY GAGA:

BEHIND THE FAME

CHAPTER 1

A STAR IS BORN

NEW YORK, 1986: THE BIG APPLE was a hive of activity, one of the most exciting, energetic and happening cities in the world. And the Reagan era was in full swing—from the drab 1970s had arisen the yuppie-driven 1980s, where nothing succeeded like excess, "greed was good," capitalism was king and opportunity abounded. It was the decade that reversed years of economic decline, witnessed the collapse of communism and rewarded success. If you wanted to go places and you worked hard enough, you would get there. In the heyday of the 1980s, before it all came crashing down a few years later, it was a joy to be alive.

One of the individuals looking to take advantage of those fast-moving times was Joseph Germanotta, who, with his wife and business partner Cynthia, was an internet entrepreneur. Back then, the internet was still in its infancy and while it was founded some decades earlier, it was not until the 1990s that the world logged onto the worldwide web and it really took off. But Joe and Cynthia, of Italian immigrant stock, were young and determined to make their mark. They planned on starting a family and were keen to raise their children in an affluent and comfortable atmosphere and they were about to succeed.

But while Stefani, as she was called before she transformed into Lady Gaga, and her younger sister Natali were brought up in cosmopolitan surroundings, their mother came from a far more parochial background: she grew up as the child of Paul and Ronnie Bissett of Glendale, Ohio. This was the heart of the American Midwest, where values are very different to those in New York: socially a very conservative environment, reliant on the old-fashioned American values of Mom and apple pie. Cynthia's own childhood could not have provided a greater contrast to the extraordinary life her daughter was to lead. But she had escaped to the big city, met Joe and was building a life for herself. Life was good and the couple began to reap the rewards of success.

Stefani Joanne Angelina Germanotta appeared on March 28, 1986, followed a few years later by her sister Natali. She was an exuberant, energetic child, and the bug to entertain bit young. "I was in the *Three Billy*

Goats Gruff when I was in kindergarten," she told one interviewer. "I was the big billy goat—I decided to make my billy goat horns out of tinfoil and a hanger." Even then, it seemed she had a flair for standing out from the crowd.

Clothes were very important to the young Stefani, just as they are now. Her love of fashion came from her mother, and by now the family was sufficiently well-off that Cynthia could have an outstanding wardrobe, full of designer names, with extravagant designs, colors and opulent elegance, which played a huge part in Stefani's life.

"She was always very well-kept and beautiful," her daughter later recalled. "She wore Ferragamo, Valentino, Paloma Picasso. . . . Her taste is absolutely classic Italian." Stefani's own taste was to prove anything but classic—her mother's early influence was, however, to stay with her into adulthood. There can be few performers who attract such attention for their unorthodox performance and her awareness of the power of clothes dates back to those days.

Indeed, one of Stefani's earliest memories is watching her mother dress and this inspired an interest that remained with her through childhood and teenage years. "It was a marvelling experience, watching her get ready for the day," she remembered on another occasion. "She always looked so much more pristine than all the other mothers. I have a lot of her in me: I went through periods where I was very sexy, then I became a hippie girl with ripped jeans, and then went into a leopard-tights-and-leotards phase, which I'm still in. Fashion saved my life! When I was young, I was laughed at in school because I dressed dramatically." But it was all preparation for what was to come. As an adult, Stefani would turn her whole life into a dramatic statement and that included her clothes as much as anything else. Indeed, she has said that the dress—or rather, *costume*—she wears when performing is often as important as the song itself. All those influences, all of that knowledge about the power of appearance, dates back to when she was still very young.

In fact, both parents had a strong influence on the young Stefani. Before he went on to earn serious money as an internet entrepreneur, Joseph himself had once played in a band and was eager to pass his love of music on to his little girl, paying for her to have piano lessons when she was still very young. Indeed, Stefani was to prove something of a child prodigy. By the age of four she had mastered the piano by ear, thus establishing very early on that music and fashion were to be her two defining features. The Stefani of four years old was already becoming Lady Gaga— albeit not quite so extreme in her tastes as the one that exists today.

Her musical education, however, was a serious

one. While she might have chosen to listen to popular entertainers, she studied the works of the great composers of the past. Her early education was, in fact, as a classically trained musician although this too went on to have great influence on her later output. Asked about the extent of that influence, she replied, "A lot! Bach and most of the classical stuff that I played when I was younger—the chord progression is the same as in pop music. It's ingrained in your sensibility about structure and discipline." This was a considerably more analytic approach to music than many of her contemporaries possessed, and one that marked her out as an entertainer for the longer term rather than just a flash in the pan.

Stefani was also a born entertainer. On her website she recalls that as a child, she sang along to songs by Michael Jackson—then at the height of his powers—and Cyndi Lauper, which she played on her mini plastic tape recorder. Nor was that all: when her parents took her out to restaurants, she would use the breadsticks as drum batons—music was clearly in the blood. She also displayed markedly exhibitionist tendencies from very early on: at home she would often greet a new babysitter stark naked. "I was always an entertainer," she said. "I was a ham as a little girl, and I'm a ham today."

As Stefani grew up, her parents really began to reap the rewards of their success. When she was seven, the family moved to an apartment in the Pythian Condominiums. Built in 1927, and converted into apartments in the 1980s, the Pythian boasts an Egyptian-themed façade and is a very upmarket residence for the city's successful business elite.

Stefani had initially been marked down to attend the prestigious Juilliard School in Manhattan. This would have been a fairly obvious choice. The Juilliard, located in the Lincoln Center for the Performing Arts, is one of the world's best-known academies for dance, drama and music. Alumni include Kevin Spacey, Robin Williams, Val Kilmer and William Hurt, among others too numerous to mention. At the last minute, however, Joe and Cynthia had a change of heart, and decided to send Stefani, aged eleven, to the Convent of the Sacred Heart. (This was the alma mater of another famous blonde, Paris Hilton.) While performance-related subjects were certainly taught there, the Convent of the Sacred Heart was another matter altogether: a very traditional and cultured institution, it was the place where the wealthy and successful of New York sent their offspring in preparation for the corridors of power in later life. It was also a sign that the Germanottas had arrived.

In later years, when Stefani burst into the limelight, a great deal was made of the fact that she attended the same school as the Hilton sisters (and it should be said that, ditzy as she might look,

Paris has been pretty sharp about building up a career of her own).

Stefani herself was rather amused by the Hilton connection. "They're very pretty, and very clean. Very, very clean," she told one interviewer, in one of her cattier interjections. "You know, I never saw Paris—she was older than me—and it's funny that the press always writes that I went to school with the Hilton sisters, but I actually only went with Nicky. Paris, I believe, left and went to Dwight. But you know, it's impressive to be that perfect all the time, these girls. I was always a weird girl in school, who did theatre and came to school with lots of red lipstick on or my hair perfectly curled, or whatever I was doing to get attention. It's funny as it's almost like they were there to make me aware, because so much of what I do now is that I try to twist my world into the commercial community so I guess they've been quite an influence on me. Not them in particular, but the idea of the self-proclaimed artist."

The Convent of the Sacred Heart was a highly select setting in which to learn and parents paid for the privilege, too. Fees for the Catholic day school were £23,000 a year and specialities included piano, dance and drama. Given that she attended this institution throughout her teens, for such an outrageous performer, Stefani came from a very conservative background: the school was initially founded in 1881 by the Society of the Sacred Heart, making it the oldest independent school for girls in New York.

Located on East 91st Street, it now occupies two huge and imposing buildings, while academic standards are extremely high. It was a very prestigious place to be educated and the other students too came from very wealthy backgrounds. The school's prom was "like a Ralph Lauren runway," recalled Stefani. "There were some quite privileged young ladies in attendance." The Convent of the Sacred Heart is also said to be the inspiration for the school in the American TV drama, *Gossip Girl*.

If Stefani was perhaps disappointed not to join the performing masses at Juilliard, as an adult she came to appreciate the start in life provided by her own establishment. "I went to a lovely school and I got an incredible education," she admitted much later on. "And I actually think that my education is what really sets me apart, 'cuz I'm very smart. I don't know that my schooling was conducive to wild ideas and creativity, but it gave me discipline, drive. They taught me how to think—I really know how to think."

And she wasn't joking about that. Stefani has come to be known for being very unusual as a performer in that she is actively involved in every single element of her shows. This attention to detail, to say nothing of the multi-faceted ability to turn her hand to all the very different disciplines required for getting a show together, was, according to the Lady herself, a direct result of her schooling. "If I decide to make a coat red in the show, it's not just red," the adult Lady Gaga went on. "I think: is it communist red? Is it cherry cordial? Is it ruby red, or is it apple red? Or the big red balloon red? I mean, there's like so many fucking different kinds of red! And so you have to say, well, what are we trying to say in this scene? Is it a happy red or a sad red? Is it a lace red, or a leather red, or a wool red? It's like there are so many components to making a show and making art, and my school taught me how to think that way."

Stefani soon began to stand out. She has since described herself as "[an] artsy, musical-theatre, nerdy girl who got good grades," who looked "a bit too sexy and a bit strange. My girlfriends used to tell me that no matter what I was wearing, even zipped up to my neck in a parka, I looked naked." That fashion sense was showing through: the costumes, both thrilling and shocking, were being rehearsed even back then. Stefani was constantly the center of attention: a combination of intelligence and charisma, allied to the desire to shock, pushed her into the spotlight.

But she was not exactly the most popular girl in school in the traditional manner, simply because she was too individual—the most popular girls tend to be those who are extremely conventional (and thus, unthreatening) and she could never be described as that. However, she had lots of friends because she was lively, interesting and clearly going places. She took part in school activities, and she pursued her own interests alongside her academic studies and made her mark on the school. In her own words, she was "focused, determined. I was always in a band, or in a musical. I didn't really fit in, but I had friends because I'm a nice girl and fun to party with."

Stefani was also from a slightly different background than her peers because although her parents were wealthy, she had not originated from socialite stock, the type of family that could trace its heritage right back to when the pilgrims first landed in New England.

"I was the arty girl, the theatre chick," she said on another occasion. "I dressed differently and I came from a different social class from the other girls. I was more of an average schoolgirl with a cork."

Given what an outrageous image she was to cultivate, Stefani's convent education was, in fact, heavy on Catholicism and morality as well as, crucially, self-discipline. Like that other Italian-American icon with whom she is so often compared (not least by Madonna herself), Stefani has always been ruthlessly determined and hardworking. According to one friend, that is what puts her in the arena for the longer term and it is also a direct result of the highly conventional education that must have seemed so restrictive at times.

"Stefani is a good girl, really sweet and normal," said Cristina Civetta, now a New York writer and fashion designer, who knew the artist back in their school days and testified to the fact that underneath all the outrageousness remains a good Catholic-Italian girl from a solid family. "She isn't from a dysfunctional family and she isn't going to burn out, like Britney Spears. Sacred Heart taught us to be very disciplined, very strong, successful women in whatever we chose as our careers, and she has chosen to be a performer."

Indeed, although Stefani might be described as something of an attention-seeker, she was nothing like as outrageous then as she came to be in later years. "We were a rich kids' school, but with good morals," Cristina continued. "Stefani was a straight-A student, who wore her skirt to her knee, as we were supposed to, and knee-high socks. I was so shocked when I first saw her perform as Lady Gaga. It was at a Lower East Side club, the Slipper Room, and she was in a coned bra and little hot pants. I said, 'Damn, you have changed!' But when we got to talking, she hadn't changed at all: she wasn't even drinking, she was still one of the nice girls. I really think her morals are still intact."

Another old friend from those days, who declined

to be named, backs up the picture of Stefani as a good Catholic girl who worked hard, did as she was told and conformed to the various strictures placed on her. "Sure, there were a few rebels," she remembered. "One girl got drunk and punched Sister Nancy so hard she knocked her out, but that was a rarity. We had to do four hours' homework each night, so there was no time for clubbing on week nights. Boys couldn't touch us; we weren't slutty. I never saw Stefani being bad—not once."

Stefani herself has admitted that all the later outrageousness was indeed, later, and back then it was mainly schoolwork and out-of-school activities. Sex was totally off the menu and would remain so for some time to come—which of course made the girls all the more attractive to the boys they came into contact with. "We were good girls, but we weren't nerdy like the girls at Chapin [another private school for girls in New York]," she said. "We were the girls that guys still wanted to date junior year of high school, because we hadn't had sex or given blow jobs yet."

Sacred Heart certainly had impressive standards of discipline, which encouraged its young ladies to behave well. "When we were dropped off at school in the morning, a Sister would greet us at the entrance and we had to curtsy to her," Cristina recalled. "In the lower school, we had to wear a grey tunic, over which we wore red-and-white checked pinafores, and blue shorts underneath everything for modesty. In the upper school, we wore blue cotton skirts in summer and a kilt in winter, and they had a yardstick to make sure they were the correct length."

Of course, while she was perfectly happy to go along with it at the time, it doesn't take a professional psychiatrist to see that Stefani's subsequent career might have been a reaction to all this. She herself maintains that, good school as it might be in many ways, in others she was held back. "Some girls were mean," she admitted on another occasion. "They made fun of me because I dressed differently. Nuns ran my school, so I was suppressing this part of myself for a long time. It wasn't until later that I realised my true passions were music, art and performance . . . definitely shock art."

Stefani might have felt that the school held her back in some ways, but it gave her an enormously useful grounding, too. She was to become mistress of her own destiny in a way that many pop stars do not: picked up by the music industry, exploited and tossed aside a few years later, performers often exercise little or no real control over their career. Stefani, on the other hand, was far more in control of what was happening around her than any other female star since Madonna. And that, in large part, was due to her schooling, for she was taught to lead and to think for herself. The nuns might turn green at the idea that they were in any way responsible for the performer that Stefani was to become, but they instilled confidence and self-belief in their young charges. Little is more vital to a successful career than those characteristics.

Incidentally, it is worth noting that the nuns were far from amused when they saw their protégée perform at the VMA Awards in 2008. Quite apart from the costume that Stefani, now Lady Gaga, was only just wearing, the lyrics she sang included, "I want to take a ride on your disco stick." It was hardly the stuff of concerts at the Convent of the Sacred Heart.

Cristina backed up Stefani's views on the quality of the school's teaching. "They blasted us with religion, but we also got an insanely good education," she said. "We had to go to mass in the chapel every Friday and a Wednesday-morning prayer meeting. There were also retreats. I attended one with Stefani for three days at a New York monastery."

Lady Gaga in a monastery is not an obvious association for those acquainted with Stefani's later work, but the retreats did not just have a spiritual dimension: they encouraged the girls to be ambitious, to plan for the future, even to take risks. After all, they were not girls who were expected to have "little jobs" until they found themselves a husband: they were to be pioneers. Stefani was encouraged to believe that she really could do anything she put her mind to, something she would prove while still very young.

"We also talked a lot at school about how we were going to be leaders," Cristina continued. "They encouraged you to try anything you wanted. When we entered the upper school, they gave us a ring with a heart that you wore facing in. To graduate, you had to write a thesis on the Arts and another on Christianity. When you graduated, you turned the ring around, showing you would take everything you had learned into the world."

In the meantime, Stefani's real talents were beginning to come to the fore. Having studied the piano almost from the moment she could walk, she was now becoming exceedingly accomplished and started experimenting with her own music when she was still very young—indeed, by the time she was thirteen, she had written her first ballad called "To Love Again." Then, from the age of fourteen, her mother would take her to New York nightclubs, such as The Bitter End By Night, where she started to learn her trade. "These were jazz bars, not sex clubs," she insisted. "They would have open-mic nights, so my mother would take me along and say, 'My daughter's very young, but she's very talented. I'll sit with her as she plays.'"

It was a very enlightened attitude to take. Both Stefani's parents took a keen interest in her career, but for her mother to accompany her to adult night-clubs must have shown an unstinting faith in her daughter's talents that blocked out any concerns she might have had. "My mom was supercool," Stefani recalled on another occasion. "She'd help me sign up and perform, and then when I got to college, I started gigging. I would ride my bike around, or walk to different clubs in New York on the Lower East Side and in the East Village. You've got to play clubs, you've got to do amazing, you've got to fail, you've got to get standing ovations and need to be booed off the stage."

At the Sacred Heart, the performing urge manifested itself in other ways too. Stefani acted in school plays, with boys from a Catholic school in the neighborhood taking the male parts, and also joined a group called the Madrigals. She also auditioned for her high school musical with the song "Speechless."

Joe and Cynthia were delighted that their daughter was showing such drive. Self-made entrepreneurs themselves, they wanted their kids to succeed and for their elder daughter to be doing so much at such a young age implied a great deal more was to come. In return, their attitude was much appreciated by their increasingly ambitious daughter for, pleased as they might have been, they were watching her take a very different path than the one they themselves had followed. Quite clearly, Stefani was heading for a show-business career rather than taking a more conventional path and yet, insecure as that world might be, they were delighted all the same.

"My parents were very supportive of anything creative I wanted to do, whether it was playing piano, or being in plays or taking method acting classes, which I did when I was eleven," Stefani said. "They liked that I was a motivated young person."

Now she was honing her artistic influences, too, some years later telling talk show hostess Ellen DeGeneres that the person she most wanted to be like was Boy George. "This is really who I am and it took a long time to be OK with that," she said, of her by-now unique style. "Maybe in high school you, Ellen, you feel discriminated against. Like you don't fit in and you want to be like everyone else, but not really, and in the inside, you want to be like Boy George— well, I did anyway. So, I want my fans to know that it's OK. Sometimes in life you don't always feel like a winner, but that doesn't mean you're not a winner if you want to be like yourself. I want my fans to know it's OK."

And Boy George was not her only musical influence. If truth be told, her accounts of school days vary wildly, for while she recognizes the benefit of the privileged education she received, her increasingly individual demeanor and appearance made her quite a handful, something she was all too aware of herself. "I was always very different and trying to not fit in too much," she admitted on *The Jay Leno Show*. "I just didn't want to be like anyone else and I was obsessed with Judy Garland and Led Zeppelin. I got really good grades—I was like a straight-A student—but I was really bad. I was very naughty, wore awful things to school. I used to roll my skirt up really high so the nuns didn't know what to do with me."

The nuns certainly didn't have many pupils like Stefani. As she advanced through teenage years, her determination to make something of herself grew; it was increasingly apparent that whatever that might be, she was not about to follow a conventional path. The Convent of the Sacred Heart might have been breeding the leaders of tomorrow, but in Stefani, they were cultivating one of the most charismatic entertainers of the early twenty-first century. They just didn't quite know what to make of it all.

Nor were matters improved by another of her growing obsessions—death: on numerous occasions, the theme has featured in her adult career, sometimes prompting alarm from certain quarters, but this too stems back to those early years. Of course, it's not unusual for teenagers to become fixated on thoughts of what might lie beyond, but in Stefani's case, she became more than usually engrossed in the subject, a fascination that would endure into adult life. "I also remembered my obsession with young women when I was younger that died, beautiful young actresses and poets. Marilyn Monroe, Judy Garland and Sylvia Plath, these young women that died, that we never saw their death," she told Ellen DeGeneres.

At the age of seventeen, Stefani won a place at New York's Tisch School of the Arts, another highly prestigious establishment and part of New York University. The establishment specializes in film, drama and dance. Tisch alumni make up the aristocracy of the show business world and include Woody Allen, Whoopi Goldberg, Angelina Jolie and Oliver Stone, among numerous others. Competition to get into the school is fierce and only a very small number of applicants are allotted a place.

Stefani was delighted to have gained her entrance, but it was now that she began to think quite seriously about what she wanted to do and where she wanted to go. In fact, for some years now she had been performing and in many ways, her time at Tisch brought matters to a head. She was on the end of conflicting advice from everyone, with no clear plan for the future and no proper idea of what she was going to do.

"It just kind of happened," she recalled afterwards. "I did theatre in high school and I did theatre in college. I went to the Tisch School of the Arts at NYU. Whenever I would do pop performances, people would say I should do theatre. When I would audition for musicals, they'd tell me I was too pop. I dropped out of college and got frustrated. I said, 'Fuck it! I will do whatever I want to do.' I started playing at the Lower East Side, then all over New York, really.

"It's funny—when I started playing in New York, when I was fourteen, it was a more folk, songwriter-y kind of show: just me and the piano. Then, when I got downtown, there were so many fucking songwriters. Everybody did the same shit, super-boring! I wanted to do something that was original and fresh. Well, there's nothing more provocative than doing pop music in the underground, instead of doing underground music that would pass as pop. I'm talking about real pop music that would pass in the underground—the reverse. So I did that."

That, of course, was still to surface. Meanwhile, Stefani was fast reaching the conclusion that Tisch, prestigious and established as it might be, was not providing her with the particular sort of experience and guidance that she wanted (if Stefani could ever be said to have "wanted" guidance) and so it was time to make a choice. After just one year, she decided to strike out on her own: now it was clear to her that she wanted to work in the music industry and, if at all possible, become a pop star. Yes, it was an extraordinarily competitive industry in which to make it, but Stefani was proving to be more than capable of standing out on her own.

And so she left Tisch, but rather than take the pop world by storm and establish herself as a hugely creative talent from the word go, Stefani very nearly messed up, even before she began. Unusually for a woman who was so clear about what she wanted, so determined and so capable, she embarked on a highly destructive period, temporarily estranging herself from her parents and putting both her health and her future at risk. A great cliché about convent girls is that when they go wild, they *really* go wild, and so it was to prove with Stefani. She might have set her heart on becoming a pop star, but that would have to wait a few years yet.

CHAPTER 2

WHEN A GOOD
GIRL GOES BAD

EW YORK, 2005: STEFANI GERMANOTTA, a nice Italian-American Catholic girl with a good education, was totally at a loose end. For the first time in her life, she wasn't working towards any particular goals, other than a vague desire to become a pop singer. What's more, she was alone. By now, Stefani had left the parental home to strike out on her own and she was living in a little apartment in New York. She had to make money somehow and so about six months after leaving Tisch, she started working as a burlesque singer to make ends meet.

Of course, this was not what Joe and Cynthia expected of her—they had brought up their girls to be functioning members of society; having sent them to a good school, they hoped the two of them would go on to have good careers. They had made something of their own lives, and to see their eldest daughter cavorting about, half-naked, was not what they looked forward to. For a time it seemed as if she was about to become another casualty of New York's club scene, with all promise well and truly lost.

Worse, far worse than that, however, was that Stefani had gotten into drugs in a big way. She started using cocaine, ordering bags of it to be delivered up to her apartment. When high, she would spend hours working on her hair and make-up. Then she would come down, snort more lines, and do it all over again. "It was quite sick," she later admitted, once out of this stage—and it was also a very dangerous way to live.

Although her addiction would not last too long, for a time it became increasingly serious. Stefani was not just a social user: she would take the drug alone, as she listened to music—the sure sign of an addict and not just a dabbler. For such an outgoing personality this was a strangely insular time: although she hadn't cut herself off from everyone as such, there were long periods of isolation, with just Stefani, her music and her drugs.

"My cocaine soundtrack was The Cure," she recalled. "I loved all their music, but I listened to this one song ['Never Enough'] on repeat while I did bags and bags of cocaine. . . . Isn't that funny? At the time I didn't think there was anything wrong with me until my friends came over and said, 'Are you doing this alone?' 'Um, yes. Me and my mirror.' And this wasn't a mirror for looking into—it was a mirror for snorting off."

Ultimately this experience would end up as a song: "Beautiful, Dirty, Rich." According to the lady herself, those years were, in some strange way, part of the performance art that was to become her life. She was, after all, carrying on the grand tradition of the tortured artist as drug user, an association that had existed for hundreds, if not thousands, of years. And by dragging herself down to the pits, she was also able to see that she didn't really want to be there. Perhaps, subconsciously, she was testing herself: did she want to destroy herself? And the answer was no.

"It's from my coke years," she said (of "Beautiful, Dirty, Rich"). "2005 was where it began, and I thought I was gonna die. I never really did the drugs for the high—it was more the romanticism of Andy Warhol and Mick Jagger, and all the artists that I loved. I wanted to be them and I wanted to live their life, and I wanted to understand the way that they saw things and how they arrived at their art. And I believed the only way I could do this was to live the lifestyle, and so I did."

There was, however, one huge difference. Some artists will take drugs because they are essentially self-destructive and intend, consciously or not, to bring about their own end; others do this to experiment and have fun. It all played a large part in Stefani's drug taking, along with feeling, somehow, that she wanted to be a creative artist, and this was how they all behaved.

"So it wasn't about getting high—it was about being an artist," she went on. "About waking up in the morning at 10:30 and doing a bunch of lines and writing a bunch of music, and staying up for three days on a creative whirlwind and then panic-attacking for a week after. It was one of the most difficult times in my life, but it was important for me to experience, since it unlocked parts of my brain. But I wouldn't encourage people to do it for that reason—you can arrive at all those things on your own."

In this short, but crucially important period, all the elements were coming together that would soon see the transformation of Stefani into Lady Gaga. Her tastes were forming and there were many other artists apart from The Cure that she was enjoying, as her taste for glam rock developed ever deeper. David Bowie was one key influence: "I used to listen to *Aladdin Sane* on the record player in my apartment," she remembered. "I'd open the window so my neighbors could hear it up the fire escape, and I'd sit out on the ledge, have a cigarette and listen. I love Bowie's voice on songs like 'Watch That Man.' I like to think I sing like a man. I want people to feel invaded when I sing, it's very confrontational."

And so it went on, the drugs, the music and the burlesque. With the benefit of hindsight, it's possible to say that this time was important inasmuch as it was to nurture some aspects of Stefani's creative output, but it certainly didn't seem like that to her parents. They had sent their daughter to a good Catholic convent school and now they had to see her in a role that seemed one step away from a stripper, while at the same time gorging herself on dangerous drugs: just what had happened to their little girl?

Joe, in particular, was appalled. He came along to see his daughter in her act, and simply couldn't believe that this was his little Stefani up there on stage. "I was performing in a leopard G-string and a black tank top," she later recalled. "He thought I was crazy. It wasn't: 'She's inappropriate' or 'She's a bad girl' or 'She's a slut'—he thought I was nuts—that I was doing drugs and had lost my mind, and had no concept of reality anymore. For my father, it was an issue of sanity."

Who could blame him? Joe and Cynthia had built up a privileged life for themselves and to see their daughter throwing it all away like that must have seemed insanity. On top of this, Stefani was an extremely talented musician, something she seemed at that point to be casually discarding too. What was the point of being an accomplished pianist if you were only going to take part in a burlesque act? Why earn a place at the Tisch just to drop out, turn off and mess up? What kind of a future was their daughter making for herself?

In fact, it was Stefani's closeness to both parents and her extremely high regard for her father that stopped her from messing up even more. Joe did not make a scene and scream over her drug taking: instead, he quite coolly laid it on the line about what would happen if Stefani kept on as she was doing. "My father is a really powerful man, a telecom guy," she explained. "So he looked at me one day and said, 'You're fuckin' up, kid.' And I looked at him and thought, 'How does he know that I'm high right now?' And he never said a word about the drugs, not one word. But he said, 'I just wanna tell you that anyone you meet while you're like this, and any friend that you make in the future while you are with this thing, you will lose.' And we never talked about it again."

But it was the wake-up call that she needed and the point was made more forcefully still by an unpleasant drug-related incident that finally brought home to her that she must stop. "I had a scary experience one night and thought I might die," she recalled. "I woke up, but it helped me become the person I am. I see things in quite a fragmented, psychotic manner, which I think is because of that. But I decided it was more important to become a centered, critical thinker; that was more powerful than the drug itself."

Even so, Joe's disapproval was such that he distanced himself from his daughter. He stopped talking to her for a while, and that was something Stefani found almost unbearable. She might have been able to take on the world in almost every other way possible, but distance from the father she adored was simply too much for her to cope with.

"As successful as people may perceive me to be, if my father called me right now and said: 'What the hell were you thinking doing this?' and was mad about something, it would break my heart," she confided, well after she became famous. "If somebody walks up to me and says, 'You're a nasty bitch, and I hate your music and you're talentless,' it means nothing to me. Nothing. But if my father says it, it means a lot.

"Eventually he came around—the record deals didn't hurt; he loves me for what I am. When I grabbed a guy today on set, he laughed. He loves it, he thinks I'm wonderful, and thank God! If he didn't, I would be a different Lady Gaga."

For all the pain of betrayal during this time, the episode also provides an insight into why Stefani had the self-confidence and the courage to do what she did. Ultimately, her parents adored her and that produced an undercurrent of self-belief that drove her to the top of one of the most competitive businesses in the world, while helping her to deal with the inevitable rejection and critics along the way. Stefani was so close to her parents that even little things, such as her choice of music were—in some circumstances—dictated by them too. She usually had a penchant for glam rock, but even here she was willing to adopt some of her father's very different tastes.

"My father is from New Jersey and he was a huge Springsteen fan," she said. "So I'm a big fan, too. 'Thunder Road' is our song. I've always loved this record, it's like a little movie." In other words, the two were extremely close.

Still, there was the minor matter of Stefani's chosen profession. She was making music, but burlesque remained the mainstay of what she was doing, something that grabbed the attention of the media when she later came to fame. "I was a burlesque dancer in New York, [but I was] never naked—unless it was by accident," she explained in one early interview. "It was performance art. I used to do it with my girlfriend, Lady Starlight. We would wear matching bikinis and go-go dance to Black Sabbath records and Metallica and Pentagram, whatever it was that we were into at the time. And light hairspray on fire!"

Lady Starlight was, indeed, shortly to come onto the scene, but before she did so, some other, early musical experimentation has since come to light. While all this was going on, Stefani was still, very slowly, beginning to pursue a musical career. She started to sing with a number of glam rock bands, including SGBand (Stefani Germanotta Band) and Mackin Pulsifer, playing in various locations in New York's Lower East Side. In the first of these gigs, she sang and played keyboards, while Eli Silverman was on guitar, Alex Beckman on drums and Calvin Pia played bass.

The group recorded a five-track demo, *Words*, with the producer Joe Vulpis: "We used to rehearse at this really dingy practice space on the Lower East Side, like, under some grocery store, where you'd have to enter through those metal doors on the sidewalk, and she had this huge keyboard that she'd wheel down the street from her apartment on Rivington and Suffolk," Calvin Pia remembered. Stefani might only have been taking mini-steps, but the process had begun.

Although Stefani was still relying on burlesque dancing to make any money, nonetheless she was progressing. In 2005, she played The UltraViolet Live, where she performed "Captivated" and "Electric Kiss." On January 20, 2006, SGBand performed at Bitter End, where the *Words* demo sold out, and in March that year, she sold *Red and Blue*, her first EP. Footage exists of one of those Bitter End gigs, with Stefani singing Led Zeppelin's "D'yer Maker," and has since been posted on YouTube: she is unrecognizable from the creature that she would later become simply because she looks so very ordinary. Her naturally brunette hair is long and slightly unkempt; she is wearing leggings and a vest, and there is even a slight hint of plumpness. But that version of the band went nowhere, drifting apart by mid-2006. Calvin Pia, who discovered the clip and posted it online, joined Akudama, while Alex Beckmann went on to Mem. Neither enjoyed quite the success of their one-time collaborator, something Pia acknowledged online.

"Before the paparazzi, Akudama's very own Calvin Pia had been blessed with the opportunity to take the stage with mega-star-to-be, Lady Gaga," began a statement on the band's website, which is where the video appeared before it made it onto YouTube. "The video might be a little toned down for all you 'Gagas' out there. The performance is as entertaining as watching Henry Fonda pick blueberries, which is honest to God, a ten out of ten by Bitter End standards. Enjoy!"

When Stefani was nineteen, she received her first, albeit brief, breakthrough. Ultimately, this would come to nothing. L.A. Reid, chairman of Island Def Jam Music Group, heard her singing in the hallway of his office and promptly signed her to Def Jam Recordings: the association was brief, given that they dropped her after three months. However,

Stefani did make a valuable contact at the time: she met the singer and producer RedOne, also signed to the label. It was to be a defining moment in her career, through both her work with RedOne, as well as the people he was to introduce her to. She might not have realized it yet, but Stefani Germanotta was well and truly on her way.

It was to prove a massive association for RedOne, too. Already he had achieved some degree of fame and success before they met, but the link-up with Stefani would propel them both into a whole different league.

"[I met her] through my management, New Heights—they used to manage her," RedOne later recalled. "Actually, at the time I started working with her she had just got dropped from her record label. My manager called me and said, 'You have to meet this girl—she is the most incredible artist.' If someone is good, it doesn't matter to me if that person has a deal. The first day we worked together, we came up with a song called 'Boys Boys Boys' and we just clicked."

RedOne was to prove one of the most important influences on Stefani's early career, going on to introduce her to Akon (of whom more later). Coming from a Moroccan and Swedish background, he too spent years struggling to gain recognition in the pop industry before his breakthrough in 2006 with a massive hit called "Bamboo," which became the official melody for the 2006 FIFA World Cup. This was, in fact, around the time he met Stefani: it was a propitious moment for both.

RedOne's background was very different from that of his new collaborator, although he displayed an equal determination. "I started playing instruments and singing at home with my family in Morocco, and when I was sixteen, I decided that this is what I wanted to do for a living," he later recalled. "Then I tried to convince my family to let me go to Sweden, because there was so much good music coming from there. When I heard the band Europe for the first time, I wanted to be a rock star. So I went to Sweden to kind of meet them. I left for Sweden when I was nineteen with my best friend. I didn't know anyone down there, so I had to start from scratch. I started studying music and played in bands."

In many ways what happened next mirrored Stefani's journey, for both she and RedOne started out as performers and then found themselves composing music for other pop stars—although in Stefani's case, of course, it would not be long before she herself was back on stage. For RedOne, however, it seemed a natural progression: he had found his métier.

"In 1995 I changed from being a guitar player and singer to the production side and then started writing for other people," he continued. "There was this producer Rami [Yacoub], who later became Max

Martin's partner. I met him at a birthday party and we kept in touch. So when I decided to become a producer, I called him up and played him songs I had been writing, and we decided to start writing together. He taught me about programming and how the software works." It was an association that was to work spectacularly well.

Right from the word go, RedOne and Stefani clicked, and although he was by far the more established of the duo at this stage, the association was always one of equals. Stefani was a trained classical musician and so she just knew what she wanted. What really happened with RedOne was that the two of them discovered that together, they were greater than the sum of their halves.

"We create things together," RedOne explained. "It's not me, it's not her, we just do it together organically from scratch. She is involved in the process from zero till the song is done. Of course she trusts me: she is a professional and that makes you become better and better, and she is so talented. Some artists can be over-the-top control freaks—that just kills the magic. With her it is not like that."

He cited as an example the way the two of them had written "Just Dance" together. "I started with the synth sequencer line, 'du du du, du du du du du . . .' and then put the chords on top and then of course the drums," he explained. "She was constantly singing while we were building the track. We put in pieces of melody here and there, and started working on the verses. Then we were thinking: what should the chorus be like? And we were singing the 'just dance' lyric. We came up with a melody, but didn't have any lyrics to it. When the label guy came in, he said, 'No, don't change anything. It's perfect like it is, it doesn't need lyrics here, just leave it—do, do, do . . . just dance.' The funny thing is, that the song was written in one hour—it was magical."

When Stefani turned twenty, she met the next major influence on her life—Lady Starlight, the DJ and fellow burlesque artiste. Lady Starlight was over a decade older and would play a crucial role in the transformation from Stefani to Lady Gaga. Like her younger protégée, she had all but created her new persona from scratch. Lady Starlight was actually born Colleen Martin, on December 23, 1975, and took on any number of personae, including DJ-ing, dancing, writing, styling and a great deal more. Like Stefani, she was heavily into glam rock; she too recognized the power of appearance and was prepared to go all out to achieve her goals. And just as Stefani would do, she chose her name because it was a song: in this case, a track by The Sweet. A highly theatrical performer, she liked to make sure her audience witnessed not just any old performance, but a happening, the memory of which would linger long afterwards. From the moment she and Stefani met, just as with RedOne, they hit it off.

And how. Indeed, it was Lady Starlight who introduced Stefani to the concept of performance art. "I actually never really thought of it like that until I started working with Lady Starlight," Stefani recalled. "One day she was like, 'It's not really a concert and it's not really a show, it's performance art. What you're doing is not just singing: it's art.' And once she pointed out to me what I was already doing, I just started analyzing that more and researching to try to take it in a different direction. And that's really what we did."

Lady Starlight herself was immediately very taken with her young charge. She saw a similar version of her younger self, and one whom she could help to mold and develop. Clearly, Stefani had great potential—she just needed a few people around her to help realise it. Ultimately, there would be a quartet: RedOne, Lady Starlight, Rob Fusari and Akon. This second, very important relationship was now beginning to form.

"I'm eleven years older than Gaga, and I do see myself as her mentor," said Lady Starlight in an interview after her young charge had broken through. "I'm Angie Bowie to her David Bowie. Angie created his look—she's my absolute hero."

Angie Bowie was, of course, married to David Bowie, and the relationship between Stefani and

Lady Starlight also contained elements of a great romance. "It was a magical connection—we were inseparable from the start," said Lady Starlight, recalling the time they first met. "I was hosting a party in Manhattan with go-go dancers and performance artists, and she was just hanging out. She had lots of ideas, and we started talking and haven't stopped since."

And the talking was about everything. There was the music, still at that point Stefani's primary concern, and then the clothes, the costumes, the performance art aspect of it all. That was when Stefani really started to work out where she wanted to go, and Lady Starlight was only too happy to take her there.

Stefani's appearance began to change quite radically now. The long brunette hair was replaced by something far blonder and tidier; the clothes began to display a provocative edge. Her music too was becoming more finely honed, while the act continued to be deliberately outrageous. In many ways, Stefani was retreating while Lady Gaga advanced—clearly, there was soon to be a massive change in her life.

Not that they had a great deal of cash to fulfill their wilder ambitions back then. "We were very creative, but the outfits were often stuck together with glue," Lady Starlight remembered. "Sometimes they fell apart when we were on stage. It was obvious even then that Gaga was going to be famous. She was incredibly focused on exactly what she wanted to do. I know she's talked about doing lots of drugs, but by the time we met she had stopped all that. She didn't even have time for boyfriends."

Almost certainly, Stefani would have made it whatever happened, but there were also some aspects of Lady Starlight's life that were to change the way she went about molding her career. For one thing, Lady Starlight had spent a lot of time in Britain and so she was very aware of the street music and fashion of the British scene. She passed that knowledge on to Stefani, who increasingly incorporated it into what she was trying to do.

"I spent two years living in London—I'd have stayed forever, if I could have got a work visa," Lady Starlight admitted. "It was there I started collecting vinyl and fell in love with the sounds of the 1970s. And I know my love of all things British rubbed off on her."

And while Stefani had already been developing her own musical tastes, Lady Starlight was introducing her to new names all the time. One favorite track was "Hey Little Girl" by the Heavy Metal Kids. "Lady Starlight introduced me to them; they're a glam-metal group who did this great song," recalled Stefani. "Glam became a big influence, it's a sub-set of all these things I love: cabaret, burlesque, metal, rock. I love Cockney Rebel, T. Rex. . . . Marc Bolan wore a full body scuba suit covered in mirrors: that's where my disco ball dress came from, when my life changed forever." Indeed, she was now standing on the brink of fame.

The two women had many other elements of their lives in common, not least their Italian heritage. And so Lady Starlight also understood quite how hard it was for Joe and Cynthia to accept their daughter's new life—although by this time they had certainly done so—because they came from a similar background and she had had to get her own parents on side, too. "They [Joe and Cynthia] are incredibly supportive," said Lady Starlight. "It was hard at first because her dad's Italian—just like mine. The last thing he wanted to see was his daughter on stage in go-go gear."

Of course, although Stefani's own career was beginning to progress beyond simply the burlesque, her on-stage costumes and off-stage outfits still owe a great deal to that time in her life. The power of burlesque lies in its ability to both shock and entertain, formative lessons that she has never forgotten and to which she still adheres to this day.

But her final breakthrough, the one that would propel her from being just another New York performer to someone who was to stand out on the global stage, was actually one of the oldest tricks in the book. No, it was *the* oldest trick in the book: Stefani discovered that sex sells.

The big moment came when she was performing

Stefani Joanne Angelina Germanotta, aka Lady Gaga, plays to the huge crowd gathered at the American music festival Lollapalooza in 2007.

Lady Gaga promoting her hit single 'Just Dance' in Sydney, Australia on 24 September, 2008.

By the end of 2008, 'Just Dance' topped the charts in six countries: Australia, Canada, the Netherlands, Ireland, the United States and the United Kingdom.

Lady Gaga is as famous for her fashion as for her music. She is instantly recognizable for her signature style: platinum blonde hair, outrageous outfits and lots of skin – even in the middle of winter!

Above: Partying with Paris Hilton at the Nokia 5800 launch party.

Below: Bombarded by paparazzi as she leaves the club.

Above: Lady Gaga in concert at G-A-Y nightclub in London at the beginning of January, 2009.

Below: She performed in front of a full house and wowed the crowd.

Her raunchy performance rocked the house as she celebrated her second week at number one with debut single 'Just Dance.'

A look that was
soon to become
her signature…
Lady Gaga and
her hair bow.

to a more-than-usually difficult audience and had to resort to desperate measures to get their attention. "I had new material and I had on this amazing outfit," she later recalled. "So I sat down, cleared my throat and waited for everyone to go quiet. It was a bunch of frat kids from the West Village and I couldn't get them to shut up. I didn't want to start singing while they were talking, so I got undressed. There I was, sitting at the piano in my underwear. So they shut up."

It was then, she says, that Stefani turned into Lady Gaga, although she had yet to adopt the name that would become famous all over the world. "That's when I made a real decision about the kind of pop artist that I wanted to be," she continued. "Because it was a performance art moment, there and then. You see, you can write about it now and it will sound ridiculous. But the truth is that unless you were in the audience in that very spontaneous moment, it doesn't mean anything. It's, like, she took her clothes off, so sex sells, right? But in the context of that moment, in that neighborhood, in front of that audience, I was doing something radical."

Perhaps. But all the years of working in burlesque, honing her act, learning her trade and linking up with the people who would help her go places was finally coming together. Stefani had had a nasty brush with the drugs world, but other than the partying she so freely admitted to, it was all over now. Just a couple of years previously, Joe and Cynthia had been concerned that their once-brilliant daughter might become just another drug-addled wreck; now something very different was about to take place. Their girl would become an internationally famous star.

But two last pieces had to be fitted into the jigsaw puzzle, and they were Rob Fusari and Akon. That latter was to prove the catalyst that sent Stefani global; indeed, he would even give her a new name. But Stefani hadn't met him yet, and hadn't yet realized quite what a huge leap she was about to make, a leap into the unknown. It would require courage, determination and talent—but she had all those and then some. She was about to transform into a bona fide star.

CHAPTER 3

THE BIRTH OF
LADY GAGA

HE STORY OF THE LIFE OF STEFANI
Germanotta, soon to become known by
a totally different name, is peopled with
child prodigies. She was one herself, as
was Rob Fusari, the songwriter who was to collaborate
on many of her most successful projects and would, in
fact, be the one to give her a new name. Like Stefani,
Rob Fusari began studying classical piano when he
was just eight, and by the time he was ten, he was
performing in national competitions. Extraordinarily
accomplished, just like his collaborator, he was used
to singing and performing from an early age, an
experience that would stand him in good stead in
later years.

"It was exciting to play in these piano competitions," he said much later. "The top three finalists
would get to play a recital at Carnegie Hall, and I had
the opportunity to play at Carnegie for three years in a

row." Manhattan's Carnegie Hall is, in fact, one of the most famous concert halls in the world. Right from the start, Fusari was accustomed to performing with the best.

He went on to study at William Patterson College in New Jersey, where he started to write songs and record demos. It was there that he made the acquaintance of someone who would go on to be a very important influence in his own life: songwriter Irwin Levine, who had been responsible for the number "Tie A Yellow Ribbon Round The Ole Oak Tree," among much else, and the two men began work together. The relationship was slightly that of mentor and mentored, another theme that was to arise more than once in the story of Lady Gaga, with Fusari learning a great deal from the older man, while Levine found inspiration from his new protégé.

"Irwin invited me over to his studio to write with him," Fusari continued. "Working with Irwin was great, I learned a lot about the craft of songwriting. We wrote together for two years, creating all kinds of music—pop, rock and country. Because Irwin was more of a lyricist, I was kind of forced into learning production and programming. We bought some gear and I jumped into it."

As he began to learn his trade, he linked up with another songwriter, Josh Thompson, and started to hone his craft still more. "Josh and I worked together for two or three years, and I got into writing R&B with him," he recalled. "I learned how to produce R&B vocals through working with Josh. We ended up writing about 300 songs together, and we would meet with labels to pitch our songs. One of the highlights was when we got to record a song with George Benson." Again, this was all experience that would be put to good use.

By now, Fusari was beginning to make his mark and his real breakthrough came when he met the producer Vincent Herbert, a slightly retiring man, but a giant in the field of pop music. As luck would have it, Herbert had just discovered a brand new group called Destiny's Child. Fusari began writing for them and as his reputation grew; he also started to compose for numerous others, including Will Smith, who was looking for a theme song for the movie, *Wild Wild West*. Further successes ensued, not least with "Bootylicious," a particular favorite of Beyoncé. Fusari was by now producing as well as writing, and he went on to work with Whitney Houston and Jessica Simpson, among others.

But it was in 2006, when he made the acquaintance of an up-and-coming young burlesque artiste, that his most famous association began. Stefani and Lady Starlight were doing their bit about town: now extremely well known on the burlesque scene, they had still to make their final breakthrough into the pop industry. Stefani, in particular, had not quite found the right sound for herself: in the end it was to be pure, unadulterated glamor pop, but she needed someone to guide her there. Fusari, meanwhile, was very receptive to new talent: he had made a conscious decision to work with developing artists, and he certainly made the right choice here.

He met Stefani, who had by this time made "Boys Boys Boys" with RedOne, signed her to a production deal and, as they were getting on with their work, an old Queen number came on the radio. "We were working one day in the studio, and Queen's 'Radio Ga Ga' came on and I was like, you are so Radio Ga Ga. So Gaga became her nickname," he recalled. He also felt there was a similarity between her voice and that of Queen's lead singer Freddie Mercury, and certainly she possessed the same flamboyance once displayed by Freddie before his untimely death in 1991.

The Lady herself remembers the occasion of her new name with fondness. "It came from the Queen song, 'Radio Ga Ga.' I used to perform at the piano, doing these really theatrical stage performances where I would do hand choreography and then slam my fingers back down on the piano, and I would wear lingerie and it was kind of like, this pop burlesque show. And he just told me, 'You're so Ga Ga, you're so Freddie Mercury.' And I was like, 'You mean Radio Ga Ga?' I just thought the name was fitting, so I kept it. He kept calling me that in the studio, so it kind of stuck."

And from that moment on, Lady Gaga is what she became. Stefani now answers to no other name and has incorporated it into a huge amount of her work (the refrain "gaga" is not uncommon in her songs). And in truth, it suits her. Quite apart from the association with Queen, another glam rock outfit, the suggestion of eccentricity is perfect for someone so innovative, so visual and so extraordinary as an artist. Not since Madonna has a woman emerged onto the pop scene so completely in charge of her own destiny and the fact that her name is as memorable as her appearance can only have helped.

The Queen connection was telling: Freddie Mercury also reinvented himself. Born Farrokh Bulsara, he was brought up in India as a Parsi and it was only after his death that many people realized that he was not European at all. Indeed, these days he is known as Britain's first Asian rock star. Lady Gaga did not play down her Italian heritage to quite the same extent, but like her namesake, she too rose above racial and national stereotypes to be herself. Neither artist can be stereotyped or put into any one box: above all, both have always been true to themselves.

Indeed, Lady Gaga actively identified closely with

Freddie Mercury, one of the greatest showmen of his generation. "I think it's part of me and what I do, there's like an androgyny to my stage show," she explained. "I'm super-feminine and sexy, but then again, I sort of carry myself like a dude. You know, the music is a reflection of who I am, and I grew up as a theatre kid and studying musical theatre and audition-ing in New York. I was a dancer, I was a singer, I was an actress: so doing theatrical pop music was a way for me to blend all of those worlds together. And Freddie Mercury was an inspiration for me when I was at a record label and they'd say 'You're too theatre,' and I'd be at an audition for a musical and they'd say, 'You're too pop'—you know? I was able to bring both worlds together."

Queen was also a big musical influence and lis-tening to the band was to help Lady Gaga find her own way. "Queen and David Bowie were the key for me," she revealed in a later interview. "I didn't know what to do until I discovered Bowie and Queen. Their songs combined pop and theatre—and that pointed a way forward."

It was exactly what she would go on to do herself.

Meanwhile, the burlesque performances, which would soon fuse into her mainstream work, continued. She was still working with Lady Starlight: now their act came to be known as Lady Gaga and The Starlight Revue. The two hosted a weekly party called New

York Street Revival and Trash Dance, with many hits from the 1970s and 80s, the era of glam rock they so loved, piling outrageous behavior on outrageous behavior—a combination of setting cans of hairspray on fire and choreographed go-go dancing certainly pulled in the crowds.

They were causing a real sensation now, at places such as Mercury Lounge, Bitter End and Rockwood Music Hall, and the two put a lot of thought into their look: "What would I be really jealous of, if I saw it in New York?" asked Lady Gaga, as she was now known to absolutely everyone. "Hot chicks in bikinis!" And so that was what they wore.

People loved it. One critic described Lady Gaga and The Starlight Revue as "the ultimate pop burlesque road show." The image, meanwhile, continued to develop. Lady Gaga was still a brunette, but she was beginning to look strikingly different from the way that she'd appeared before: "When I started out, I was pretty funky, but not quite so mad," she later recalled. "I wore a leotard and had my hair like Amy Winehouse. I would sing and play the piano while wearing a hundred orchids in my hair. I was a real flower child, but quite sweet with it. As I got older, the show got more over-the-top. I'd be go-go dancing in front of fifteen people who didn't know who I was, but I'm a fearless person, although I shudder now when I look back at how naive I was."

But it was all grist to the mill, later to be incorporated into the mainstream. It also meant that Lady Gaga had no fear of nudity either, which was fortunate given that it was to feature so heavily in her work.

The girls were beginning to expand their horizons, too, venturing further afield and not only performing in New York, as they had done initially. The rest of the United States was beginning to wake up to their charms. Writing in *Seattle Weekly*, Erika Hobart was witness to one of their shows: "Earlier this year a relatively unknown artist named Lady Gaga (Stefani Germanotta) stormed into Neighbors unannounced, infiltrating the club with a set that sounded like a mash-up of Billy Idol, Madonna, and Peaches spun by a drunk DJ," she wrote. "She wore a platinum blonde wig and a red American Apparel outfit so tight it could trigger a yeast infection. She looked like Ziggy Stardust in hooker heels and electrified the crowd. 'Pop music will never be lowbrow—at least not on my stage,' Gaga concluded with a smirk."

That early review testified to another characteristic that is crucial in becoming a star: charisma and stage presence. Lady Gaga could never be accused of being a shrinking violet, but well before she set the world alight, she could still dominate a stage. And dominate she did with her exuberant costumes, outrageous performances and general fearlessness: she was giving the impression that she was ready to take on the world, and conquer it, she did.

At the same time, she was getting into dance music, too. "I was in New York, partying a lot at gay clubs and dive bars," Lady Gaga recalled in an early interview with *Rolling Stone Magazine*. "I was out five nights a week. I fell in love with The Cure, the Pet Shop Boys, the Scissor Sisters; I got really fascinated with Eighties club culture. It was a natural progression from the glam, Bowie-esque, singer-songwriter stuff I'd been working on. I used to take my demo into clubs, but I would lie and say that I was Lady Gaga's manager, and that she was only available to play on Friday nights at 10:30—the best time slot."

People were really sitting up and taking notice now. Lady Gaga had started to attract the attention of the gossip columnists, not least the highly influential gossip blogger Perez Hilton, who were only too delighted to put news of her outrageous antics and appearances all over their websites, thus providing inestimable publicity at a time when everything was falling into place. Indeed, Perez Hilton can claim a huge role in introducing her to a wider public: a lover of divas himself, Lady Gaga was exactly his kind of girl. And she gave him plenty of material, too: always aware of the importance of appearance, her increasingly outrageous outfits cropped up, time after time, on his website: the cult of Lady Gaga was almost ready to take off.

As they increasingly attracted even more attention, Ladies Gaga and Starlight were asked to perform at the Lollapalooza annual music festival, just outside Chicago, and what started out as being simply a good opportunity turned into an even greater publicity vehicle than anything that had gone before. Lollapalooza was a good showcase in itself: running intermittently since 1991, it featured all kinds of music, dance and comedy performances, with a little politics thrown into the mix. It also played a part in popularizing many acts, including Pearl Jam, Red Hot Chili Peppers and Hole, and it was to do the same for the upcoming star, only Lady Gaga's appearance at the festival didn't quite go according to plan.

In early interviews, when Lady Gaga spoke of her appearance at Lollapalooza, she was uncharacteristically coy about what stood out about the event and instead concentrated on the technical and artistic aspect of it all. "It was a blast," she told one reporter. "I mean, it was a bit nerve-wracking—we had tremendous technical difficulties on the stage. That was not a performance that I choose to really remember so fondly. But if anything, what I loved the most about it was that the sea of hippies and so forth that were there were not expecting what they saw, and I loved the shock art aspect of it. Actually, I'm hoping to incorporate some pretty interesting things into the show that capture their reactions and stuff. You'll see more of that in the future."

From the word go, Lady Gaga had been shocking audiences, but now she really was beginning to learn how to grab a crowd's attention and milk it for all it was worth. What she seemed a little more reticent about—to begin with, at least—was the fact that she'd got arrested. There was certainly no reason for embarrassment (sometimes the danger of arrest seems to go with the territory in the life of a pop star) and the cause of the arrest, indecent exposure, was pretty much what she was basing her act around. Nonetheless, in the wake of the affair, she sounded extremely indignant.

"I was outside the Lollapalooza festival in Chicago and this policeman came up and told me my hot pants were too short," she told one interviewer. "They weren't really pants at all, but he got upset and I got a citation. All people will have seen is this half-naked girl on the street yelling, 'It's fashion! I'm an artist!'"

In another interview, she continued to be indignant. "It's a music festival," she protested. "Everyone was doing drugs. I think my girlfriend actually had drugs in her pocket. And they arrested me for wearing hot pants? It was ridiculous."

Perhaps so, but it did her reputation no harm at

all. During her Blonde Ambition Tour, Madonna was threatened with arrest by the Canadian authorities for simulating masturbation and it certainly didn't hinder her career in the long term, but simply generated acres of publicity, thus enhancing the image of a maverick. Lady Gaga's arrest was in similar vein—as her fame grew, the world grew fascinated by every aspect of her personality and the whole episode just added to her mystique.

That reference to "my girlfriend" was, of course, Lady Starlight. Lady Gaga has always professed to be bisexual, although according to her, her feelings for women are only physical and not emotional. It's hard to judge just how far their relationship went in amorous terms, and how much of it was an act. After Lady Gaga hit the big time, numerous pictures of the two women fondling each other emerged, but the fact is, they were burlesque artists then and that is what such performers do. Indeed, the relationship seems to be more that of mentor and mentored than any fiercely sexual flame.

According to the lady herself, men tended to be slightly put off by the more Sapphic aspects of her personality. "The fact that I'm into women, they're all intimidated by it," she once said. "It makes them uncomfortable. They're like, 'I don't need to have a threesome—I'm happy with just you.' I have no question in my mind about being bisexual. I think people are born bisexual and they make subconscious choices based on the pressures of society." In this, incidentally, she had yet something else in common with Madonna, who at one stage also cultivated a bisexual image, most notably with the comedienne Sandra Bernhard although the relationship never really seemed to take off.

But as far as Lady Gaga was concerned, her only really serious relationship at that stage had been with a heavy metal drummer called Luke. That was over by now, having caused her some considerable pain in the process—"I was his Sandy, and he was my Danny, and I just broke," she said, referring to the lead characters in the musical *Grease*—although the romance was to inspire some of her early output. Luke was the inspiration behind much of the work on her debut album, *The Fame*, from "Boys Boys Boys" to "Paparazzi," but she had pretty much recovered from it now. And given the way her career was going, she might have been forgiven for having more on her mind than love.

That said, the men in her life had been a huge influence on her music. Lady Gaga has revealed that she wrote "Boys Boys Boys" in order to impress a man: "Yeah, that's the kind of way I think of boys," she said. "I dunno, maybe I'm just a different kind of girl, but the first love of my life used to drive me around in an El Camino. It's watermelon-green with a black hood, and he has long, jet-black hair and he looks like half Neil Young, half Nikki Sixx when they were young, and the way that he talks about his car . . . and the way that he stalls the gas when he's turning the corner . . . that's my guy!

"I like guys like that, guys that listen to AC/DC and drink beers, and buy me drinks just to show me off at the bar by the jukebox with their friends. That's kind of like an old hot groupie chick."

It was a side to her that she didn't let out much, a direct result of her upbringing. "I don't think a lot of female pop stars embrace womanhood in that domestic, American way," she continued. "And me singing about gasoline and car and beers and bars is very American. I lurrrrrve Springsteen, grew up listening to Springsteen! And it's like that sort of by-the-boardwalk mentality. Girls either don't know about it or they think no one can relate to it, or they think it's cooler to act like men and cheat on their boyfriends and yunno. They're, 'I don't want plastic surgery! Fuck plastic surgery! And fuck cooking you dinner, I'm gonna fucking order in!' And I'm not like that—I used to make my boyfriend dinner in my stilettos, with my underwear on. And he used to be like, 'Baby, you're so sexy!' And I'd be like, 'Have some meatballs.'"

Well, she didn't have time for that now. Indeed, Lady Gaga had not merely been busy with Lady

Starlight: she was working hard with Rob Fusari, too. By now, the two had produced enough material to show someone else, and so Rob took their collaboration to Vincent Herbert—the man Lady Gaga always credits with having discovered her—who immediately spotted her potential. He signed her to the newly formed Streamline Records, an imprint of Interscope Records—but as a songwriter, not a singer, a role for which she was clearly qualified, having already done some work for Famous Music Publishing. And the experience was to stand her in very good stead. "She interned at Famous Music Publishing before any of this," recalled Jody Gerson, post-*The Fame*, who signed her to a publishing deal with Sony/ATV. "And even back then, she was famous for showing up for work in her undies."

Lady Gaga herself was delighted by this turn of events. "Getting into writing for others happened naturally, because at the time, I didn't have a record deal," she explained in an interview with *Billboard Magazine*, shortly after the release of her first album. "I had a deal with IDJ that came and went, but that was it. I don't have an ego about other people singing my songs." Nor should she—if she'd stuck to that field alone, she would still have been an enormous success.

Herbert himself was delighted with his new find. And once she got going, she really did so: "She wrote almost all her hits in a week," he recounted admiringly after the first album release. "She flew to LA and sat in a studio with RedOne and just cranked it out."

Lady Gaga's self-discipline and work ethic were beginning to pay off. Ironically, given how worried he'd been about her earlier drug use, she was now showing herself to have exactly the same drive as her father revealed when building up his own business: she saw the opportunity in front of her, and she went for it. Sometimes, it's all too easy to forget that behind the frequently bizarre appearance, the brashness, the urge to outrage and all the bling lurks a truly formidable business brain: by the time Lady Gaga hit the big time, nothing had been left to chance. Her assault on the music business was meticulously planned: she found what suited her and proceeded to take the world by storm.

She took her work quite seriously, too. "I have a fascination with Andy Warhol and the way he wanted to make commercial art that was taken as seriously as fine art," she explained. "Music has gotten so pretentious that now it's almost rebellious to be a pop artist. A lot of indie-rock bands and singer-songwriters have this middle finger up at the pop world and record labels. There's been a lot of damage done over the past 30 years, with artists saying that pop music sucks. It's lowbrow, manufactured, fake, plastic. They say we need to go back to the 'real music,' so we've had to listen to some really depressing singer-songwriters and indie-rock bands."

But there was nothing depressing about what she was planning to do. Lady Gaga wanted to make good, catchy pop music, and that is exactly what she went on to do. She was totally pragmatic about it as well. "A hit record writes itself," she continued. "If you have to wait, maybe the song isn't there. Once you tap into the soul, the song begins to write itself. And I usually write the choruses first, because without a good chorus, who really gives a fuck? I think most music is pop music. The mark of a great song is how many genres it can embody. It's about honesty and connection—look at a song like 'I Will Always Love You.' Whitney killed it as a pop song, but it works as a country song, a gospel song, everything. If I can play a song acoustic, or just on the piano and it still works, I know it's good."

And she was now writing fast. She signed the deal with Sony/ATV Music and started writing for some of the biggest names of the day, artists such as Britney Spears, New Kids On The Block, Fergie and Pussycat Dolls. And, different as they might have been in their image, Lady Gaga and Britney proved a match made in heaven. Both were disco queens, both were mesmeric on stage and while the more junior member of the partnership, Lady Gaga, was also perhaps the most talented one, she was wise enough to play it down at the time.

Indeed, from the word go, she has never had anything but good things to say about Britney. "It was awesome seeing the song change when she put her touches on it," she recalled of "Quicksand," a hit she wrote around the time of Britney's so-called comeback after a series of very public personal problems. "I'm just really grateful that she loves the music and she's so supportive of me. She's a fan of my stuff, and to write a song that she loves and to know she loves me as an artist, you can't ask for anything better than that.

"Britney's a real class act in terms of the way she handles herself in the media and embraces new artists. She's always really kind—I've always admired that about her. She's gonna kick everybody's ass, she's awesome! As far as I'm concerned, Britney never left."

This was pretty big-time stuff. For all that Lady Gaga had become a fixture on the New York burlesque scene, Britney Spears was an international A-lister: to be so closely associated with her was a huge leap forward. And while Lady Gaga has always put herself forward as being too cool for school, she couldn't help but sound thrilled by the association—"I used to go to TRL with my girlfriends after school sometimes just to see Britney's fingernail in the window," she admitted. "I've gotta say 'Slave 4 U' [Britney's most recent single at the time of the interview] was a moment for everyone. When that bitch came out with that slammin' body and that sweaty video, we were all, like, 'We can't hate on you!' She ended every pop diva's life, it's a good video."

Perez Hilton backed that one up: he published a page from Lady Gaga's senior high school yearbook, which not only had her claiming her male equivalent was Boy George, but also that she was separated at birth from . . . Britney Spears. The only unusual thing about this blog, incidentally, was that Lady Gaga looked so ordinary: she was back in her brunette days, a typical longhaired teenager. Now very peroxide indeed, she was almost unrecognizable from the child she'd once been.

But to work with Britney! Lady Gaga loved Britney and Britney, at least, liked Lady Gaga—she was showing none of the jealousy and rivalry with which an established artist so often greets someone new. "She's a nice girl—I just feel very honored that she wanted to sing my song," said Lady Gaga on another occasion. "I used to scream for her in Times Square and now I work for her! When I was thirteen, she was the most provocative performer of my time. I love her so much! [But] Britney certainly doesn't need any freakin' tips from me! Britney Spears is the Queen of Pop. I was learning from her."

She was also to pay her the ultimate tribute—flashing a few seconds of Britney's "I Love Rock 'N' Roll" on screen during a live performance.

Even so, Lady Gaga was well aware of the differences between them. Britney was a sex kitten, albeit a very talented one, whereas she was something else altogether, a look she defined for herself. "I am not sexy in the way that Britney Spears is sexy—which is a compliment to her because she's deliciously good-looking," she explained. "I just don't have the same ideas about sexuality that I want to portray. I have a very specific aesthetic—androgyny. I just have a very specific way of seeing things, it's supposed to be different from everybody."

She was similarly enthusiastic about the other artists that she was writing for. Indeed, she would go on to tour with both New Kids On The Block and Pussycat Dolls. Meanwhile, the final piece of the jigsaw was about to slip into place—and that was Akon.

Akon, aka Aliaune Badara Akon Thiam, is a Senegalese-American singer songwriter and producer. He had his own breakthrough in 2004, following the release of the single "Locked Up" from his first album *Trouble,* and went on to receive a Grammy award nomination for the single "Smack That" from his second album, *Konvicted.* Following this, he founded two record labels, Konvict Muzik and Kon Live Distribution, and in a staggeringly successful career has since become the first solo artist to twice hold the number one and two slots on the Billboard Hot 100 charts. He has also been nominated for six Grammy awards and has developed an eye for spotting new talent—which is where Lady Gaga came in.

It happened, as these things so often do, almost by accident. Lady Gaga was already doing very well as a songwriter: Interscope loved her; she was forming good relationships with colleagues and clearly had an extremely commercial sound. Of course, she was a trained musician herself, but at that stage no one thought she might make it as a front-of-house singer: she was still very much a behind-the-scenes girl. But then, Lady Gaga sang one of the songs that she had penned for another artist, just as a reference vocal, and Akon got to hear it. Moreover, he liked what he heard.

Matters, again, began to move fast. Akon recognized straight away that here was a major new talent: he spoke to Jimmy Iovine, chairman and CEO of Interscope-Geffen-A&M, and managed to convince him to sign Lady Gaga to his own label, Kon Live Distribution. This was towards the end of 2007. And Lady Gaga did not hang about: she and RedOne hit the studio and after just one week had amassed an enormous collection of new material, including two songs that would go on to become massive international hits,

"Just Dance" and "Poker Face."

"I was like the weird girl who dressed like a zoo animal, the trash glamor in a roomful of urban hip-hop cats," she later recalled. "They'd be, like, 'Gaga, what do you think of this lyric?' and I'd twist it all up, and all of a sudden it was edgy."

But that wasn't all. She also worked with the producer and songwriter Martin Kierszenbaum, collaborating on four songs, including "Eh, Eh (Nothing Else I Can Say)." Kierszenbaum had established another Interscope imprint, Cherrytree Records, and Lady Gaga also joined the crowd of artists on that particular label. Now it really was just a matter of time.

Akon, whose nose for new talent rarely proved more astute, was loving every minute: although others had discovered her as a songwriter, it was he who realised that Lady Gaga's real place was at the center of the action—and how. She wasn't just rising to the challenge, she was taking every opportunity that came her way, shaking it by the neck and extracting every last little bit of juice from it. His new signing was extraordinary; she really was the most amazing find.

"She's incredible," Akon told MTV news in the wake of her debut album, *The Fame*. "That's my franchise player at the moment. Gaga's been so incredible, I think she's a magnate to the industry in general. She's brave, she's fresh, she's different; she's bold, she don't give a damn! You gotta take her as she is, that's the beauty of it. You're forced to like her the way she is without no extra stuff added. She's like a sister to me. That's like my girl. She's right here, in a headlock!"

Akon was also to prove an invaluable ally when Lady Gaga and her record label discussed the kind of sound they wanted to come out. Initially, there were fears that what she was putting out was not mainstream enough, but she held her ground and at first managed to have her way. "They would say, 'This is too racy, too dance-oriented, too underground. It's not marketable,'" she revealed in an interview in 2009. "And I would say, 'My name is Lady Gaga, I've been on the music scene for years, and I'm telling you, this is what's next.' And look—I was right."

And the story really had only just begun.

CHAPTER 4

THE FAME

Y THE BEGINNING OF 2008, LADY GAGA HAD moved full-time to LA. She was a native New Yorker, born and bred in one of the greatest cities in the world— "I am New York, I'm a hustler—I ate dust since I was fifteen, and I kept going even when I was told no"—but she needed to live under the Californian sun to work on her career. And so she went, and in doing so, she was about to hit the big time in an incredible way.

One of the first things Lady Gaga did was to assemble a collective known as the Haus of Gaga (that alone should have been warning enough that this was no ordinary star), who worked with her on every aspect of the music, be it her shows, her clothing, the music itself or whatever was deemed worthy of attention. It was very reminiscent of Andy Warhol's Factory, as she herself acknowledged, bringing together a pool of talent and channelling it in one direction. "In this industry, you get a lot of stylists and producers thrown at you, but this is my own creative team, modelled on Warhol's Factory," she explained. "Everyone is under twenty-six and we do everything together."

And they all took it seriously: "How do I make pop, commercial art be taken as seriously as fine art? That's what Warhol did. How do I make music and performances that are thought-provoking, fresh and future? We decide what's good, and if the ideas are powerful enough, we can convince the world that it's great."

And they were certainly about to do that. Intensive work had been done on the first album— Lady Gaga was just as determined as her record label that she would make the most enormous splash. It was to be called *The Fame* (post-modern irony, perhaps, but a prediction as well) and combined genres, according to the artiste herself, "from Def Leppard drums and hand-claps to metal drums on urban tracks."

Meanwhile, she was out there, making herself known. "I did it the old-fashioned way," she explained in the wake of the release of her first single, when she suddenly became famous almost overnight. "I played every club in the US, shook hands and thanked every DJ for spinning my music profusely, while they got drunk. I have a relationship with the underground dance community as a pop artist, that's not something everybody gets."

The debut single was to be a number called "Just Dance," which was released on April 8, 2008. Written by Lady Gaga and produced by RedOne, it also featured vocals from Akon and Gaga's labelmate, Colby O'Donis. It was, she said, a "happy record," mainly about drinking too much and clubbing. The accompanying video, with Lady Gaga sporting a very David Bowie-esque lightning streak down one cheek, had her turning the song on and persuading fellow revellers to get up and dance. As a proclamation of intent towards the dancers of the world, it was to be spot on.

"I was very hungover," she later recalled. "I wrote the song in about ten minutes with RedOne. And it was my first time being in a Hollywood studio—very pristine, big huge room with giant speakers."

She was obviously revelling in her new life. This was to be her first big production music video (although in truth, it paled in comparison with what was to come) and featured cameos by Akon, Space Cowboy and Colby O'Donis.

"Oh it was so fun, it was amazing," she told one journalist. "For me it was like being on a Martin Scorsese set. I've been so low-budget for so long, and to have this incredibly amazing video was really very humbling. It was really fun, but you'll see if you ever come to a videoshoot of mine one day—I'm very private about those things, I don't really talk to everybody. I'm not like the party girl running around, I might even seem to be a bit of a diva. I'm sort of with myself, in my work headspace worrying about costumes, and if extras look right, and placement. I don't just show up for things, you know.

"That video was a vision of mine. It was Melina the director who wanted to do something, to have a performance art aspect that was so pop, but it was still commercial, but that felt like lifestyle. It was all those things, I love it."

The record-buying public loved it too, as did the critics. It was "galactic," pronounced Matthew Chisling of Allmusic. The song "opens the album like a valkyrie leading the charge, riding triumphant ahead of her army," said Ben Norman of About.com. "If you don't know this song, use your browser. I won't waste time explaining what it sounds like."

"You won't get many more catchy party odes than the chart-topping 'Just Dance' this year, a polished gem set to lodge in your head for the next few weeks," wrote Ben Hogwood in MusicOMH.com. "[It is a] beguilingly compulsive tale of pulling a drug-induced whitey, with a combination of clipped marching beats, sawing electronics and mild R&B flavour that bears a vague resemblance to Nelly Furtado's 'Maneater,'" said Alex Petridis in the *Guardian*. And so it went on.

"Just Dance" turned out to be a massive hit, but not in quite the way anticipated. Appropriately, given the background from which Lady Gaga had emerged, clubbers absolutely loved it. To begin with, it became a cult sensation, finding its way onto the Billboard charts and staying there. But it was only months later, in January 2009, that the song finally reached the top of the charts, having become the music world's best-kept secret, before eventually making it into the mainstream—much like its creator. In total, it took 22 weeks to reach the top, ultimately selling 3 million in the United States alone.

World domination had begun. First, it was just the club scene, but then mainstream culture began to take notice of this extraordinary creature, who seemed to have landed fully realized as a pop star with the most extraordinary visual ability in the midst of Planet Celebrity from somewhere in outer space. In truth, given some of the outfits she presented herself in, Lady Gaga looked like an alien; at other times she came across as a real beauty. The world was entranced, while she herself was lapping it up. She was utterly unlike anyone or anything else out there on the pop scene, and she knew it, too.

"I'm defying all of the preconceptions we have of pop artists," she said, and she was right there. "I'm very into fashion—I channel Versace in everything I do. Donatella is my muse in so many ways: she's iconic and powerful, yet people throw darts at her. She's definitely provocative, and I channel that more so than anything else."

"Provocative" didn't begin to describe this strange new creature. All the dancing meant that Lady Gaga had a beautiful figure, which she was not afraid to show off, at times almost appearing to regard clothes as optional. Nor was she some bimbo: this was an extremely clever, classically trained pianist, who had spied an opening in the market and was prepared to use it to the full.

"I'm filling an enormous hole," she declared. "There's a wide-open space for a female with big balls to fill! I'm here to make great music and inspire people."

Work continued on *The Fame*, which was due to be released in August 2008. In the meantime, Lady Gaga was starting to tour: she had written tracks for New Kids On The Block's comeback album *The Block*, and now she planned to tour with them as their warm-up act. And she was just as enthusiastic as she had been about Britney: "I wrote a song on the album and I'm a featured singer on a song called 'Big Boy, Big Girl,'" she told one reporter. "The album will surprise people. It's completely futuristic—new, now and contemporary. There is nothing jaded or old about it; it's them doing 2008. Working with them is the most incredible experience—they are just an amazing talent. It is going to be a good year for them; I have faith that they are really going to come back with a bang."

Indeed, the impact was such that it was reported on Reuters:

SANTA MONICA, Calif., Oct. 3 2008 – Pop star
Lady Gaga is embarking on her first ever tour,
opening up for the sold-out reunion New Kids
On The Block tour, one of the biggest tours of the
fall. The New York native will begin her stint
with NKOTB in Los Angeles on October 8, and
will continue through the end of November.

Lady Gaga exploded onto the music scene this
summer with her global hit "Just Dance." The
pop smash has made the Top 10 in 14 countries,
and earlier this year she performed it in front of
over a billion viewers on The Miss Universe
Pageant. The singer-songwriter's debut album,
The Fame, will be released on October 28.

Just as she had been in the States, Lady Gaga was
now being noticed in Britain. People were starting to
catch on to the fact that here was a major new talent in
their midst and predicted great things: "You'll go Gaga
over Lady Gaga," wrote Dan Wootton in the *News Of
The World*. "This American pop genius will be huge.
Her dance-pop and electronica is superb and will melt
the UK charts early next year." His prediction proved
absolutely correct.

Naturally, Lady Gaga was garnering not just
acclaim, but also controversy. Her frequently semi-
naked appearances, to say nothing of sexually explicit
imagery, upset some of the more conservative elements

in society but just like Madonna, two decades previously, not only was she utterly unrepentant, but she absolutely revelled in it.

"If people think Gaga is over-the-top and decadent now, I'm afraid for them, they have no idea what's to come," she predicted accurately. "I eat, sleep, breathe and bleed every inch of my work. I'd absolutely die if I couldn't be an artist."

But she was an artist, and then some. Lady Gaga was beginning to make serious money, but that was not, she said, what it was all about: "Some artists are working to buy the mansion or whatever the element of fame must bear, but I spend all my money on my show," she declared. "I don't give a fuck about money! What am I going to do with a condo and a car? I can't drive." It was money well spent, however, for the show became more impressive by the day.

In September 2008, with "Just Dance" still dominating the charts, came the release of the second single from the album: "Poker Face." This went on to reach number one in nearly twenty countries, proving once and for all that there really was a major new name on the scene. It was another dance number, but also a further upset to the conservative element, for its theme was rather darker (and more provocative)—namely bisexuality and gambling. Nor did the accompanying video attempt to calm matters down: it featured Lady Gaga playing strip poker.

Now the world really started to get a taste of what this vibrant new pop star was like. "I like boys that look like girls," she began. "All my boyfriends look like Nikki Sixx, amazing." she added. "But something I don't really talk about is if you listen to the chorus, I say, 'He's got me like nobody' then 'She's got me like nobody.' It's got an undertone of confusion about love and sex."

At that point, she stopped short, without actually going on to talk about bisexuality, instead moving the subject on to music—"I love church music, Church and Mass in general, it's like a play. I really enjoy it," she continued, before betraying one note of insecurity: "I was told for a very long time that I was not pretty enough, too strange, not edgy enough. But I've always been famous—it's just that nobody knew."

In interviews, she veered between the straight and the bi, again further increasing the interest in her, wherever she went. On one occasion it was all about boys: "It's about a lot of different things," she explained. "I gamble, but I've also dated a lot of guys who are really into sex and booze and gambling, so I wanted to write a record my boyfriends would like too." But then she sharply changed tack, telling concert-goers that the song is actually about a woman who is with a man, but fantasizes about being with a woman—hence the man has to read her "poker face." The audience lapped it up.

Lady Gaga was having a lot of fun. In an interview with *Rolling Stone Magazine*, she was asked what exactly the line "Bluffin' with my muffin" meant? "Obviously, it's my pussy's poker face!" she replied brightly. "I took that line from another song I wrote, but never released, called 'Blueberry Kisses.' It was about a girl singing to her boyfriend about how she wants him to go down on her, and I used the lyric: 'Blueberry kisses, the muffin man misses them kisses.'"

In similar vein, she was also asked to explain "I wanna take a ride on your disco stick," from the track "LoveGame." "It's another of my very thoughtful metaphors for a cock," said Lady Gaga, who was, more than ever, proving herself to be nobody's fool. "I was at a nightclub, and I had quite a sexual crush on somebody, and I said to them, 'I wanna ride on your disco stick.' The next day, I was in the studio and I wrote the song in about four minutes. When I play the song live, I have an actual stick—it looks like a giant rock-candy pleasuring tool—that lights up."

"Poker Face" was not just a huge commercial success: the critics loved it, too. It was one of the best tracks on the album, said Priya Elan from *The Times*, with its "love as card game cheek." "'Poker Face' works well on pop radio, but with slight mixing alterations it would be equally at home in a dark, sweaty, late-night party atmosphere," enthused Bill Lamb of About.com. "She has refreshed the pop world in the US and UK at one of the slowest times of the year. 'Poker Face' keeps the motors humming as everyone waits for the next step forward from Lady Gaga." That was surely something—this was only her second single and already the world hotly anticipated the next.

Meanwhile, in *Billboard*, Chris Williams wrote: "Once again, hooks are aplenty, with '80s-inspired synthesizers, robotic verses and a warm, sunny hook in the chorus, which is even more addictive than the previous single. With a focused artistic vision, a swagger in her interview style, and above all, a fantastic collection of diverse pop nuggets, Gaga is playing her cards right—and Poker is another obvious ace." And there was a great deal more of the same.

"Poker Face" ended up at Number One on the Hot 100, as had "Just Dance," which meant that Lady Gaga was the first artist to have had number one hits with her first two songs since Christina Aguilera achieved the same thing in 1999/2000 with "Genie In A Bottle" and "What A Girl Wants." She became the first singer to top all three dance charts since Madonna's "Sorry" in 2006 and the first artist in digital musical history to top the four million mark in paid downloads with just two songs.

The accompanying video was just as polished as its predecessor. It was filmed at a luxury villa on the betting company bwin's PokerIsland (bwin also provided the poker equipment, for which it received product placements), starting out at the pool from which Lady Gaga emerges, wearing a mirrored masquerade mask and a black leotard, accompanied by two Great Danes (for Gaga trivia fans, they were a mother and son called Lava and Rumpus).

Lady Gaga then whips off her mask and starts singing as she dances in the mansion and beside the pool, by now wearing a turquoise leotard, before a strip-poker party begins. Everyone gets down to their underwear and starts making out: while this is clearly an orgy scene, even she couldn't take it any further and so some decorum is preserved. As it was, the words "muffin," "Russian Roulette" and "gun" were frequently bleeped out, offending, as they did, various people's more delicate sensibilities. Still, it was a triumph.

Lady Gaga herself was delighted with the decidedly raunchy end result. "I knew I wanted it to be sexy, so I thought no pants, because that's sexy, and I knew I wanted it to be futuristic, so I thought shoulder pads, because that's my thing," she explained. The quality of the work said a lot about her, too. Not only was the song a great dance track, everything about it and the accompanying video was so polished. Nothing had been left to chance here: both Lady Gaga and Interscope were determined to achieve pop perfection, and they did.

In fact, "Poker Face" became an instant pop classic. Rapper Kid Cudi's single, "Make Her Say," had a vocal sample from the acoustic version (indeed, his own track was originally titled "I Poke Her Face," but was changed to get radio play), featuring Kanye West. Kanye was a big fan of Lady Gaga's—who wasn't? But the song was slightly changed to take out the bisexual references. "When I saw that YouTube [video], that's what made me fall in love with the song—when I saw her play the acoustic version," he recalled. "I could hear all the melody lines. On the 'Poker Face' single, she sings it straightforward, almost, like, ripping it or chanting it. But this [acoustic version], you hear the Broadway melodies run up and down. I was inspired by that; I wanted to sample it. I thought it was really dope—just on some hip-hop, 'Say when I p-p-poke her face.'"

Lady Gaga loved the new version, saying that Kanye West had seen what it was really about. "It's funny, because a lot of my fans were like, 'Gaga, Kanye wrote a song and it's not about what your record's about. Your record is about gambling and this song is about dirty sex things,'" she said. "I said to them, 'You're wrong: Kanye was right.' That's exactly what this song is about. The record is about how I used to fantasize about women when I was with my boyfriend. It was, like, really exciting that he had so much insight into what the song was about. He's a cool guy."

Meanwhile, she was gaining more fans still. The *Guardian* compared her to a "smutty Gwen Stefani," while the *Sunday Times* said, "A screwed-up Britney via BoomBox, who once went to school with Paris Hilton, the Lady is all sequined knickers, catchy Kylie-style tunes and the pottiest of mouths. . . ." She was seen as the new leader of a group of female singers that was taking over the previously male-dominated field of electropop, a role she was only too happy to assume: "It's a good time now," she agreed. "There's a big empty space that was waiting to be filled by women."

She cited Andy Warhol again, "because of his ability to take commercial art and create an intellectual and artistic space, where it was taken seriously. The idea is to make things—videos, fashion, performance art—which are innately significant and insignificant, that will cause argument: 'Is Lady Gaga valid or invalid?'"

It was then announced that she would tour with another group that she had previously been writing for, the Pussycat Dolls. Practically every newspaper cited her as a name to watch in 2009. It was also said that Christina Aguilera was copying Lady Gaga's look, which really did not go down well with the more established diva: "You know, that's funny that you mention that," she said, rather coolly, to one interviewer. "This person was just brought to my attention not too long ago. I'm not quite sure who this person is, to be honest. I don't know if it is a man or a woman, I just wasn't sure. I really don't spend any time on the internet so I guess I live a little under a rock in that respect. I've been in this business so long there's always some comparisons." Reading between the lines, the accusation stung.

In fact, it actually caused a mini-scandal at the time and Lady Gaga played a blinder. "Well, it was very flattering when it happened," she remarked. 'She's such a huge star and if anything, I should send her flowers because a lot of people in America didn't know who I was until that whole thing happened. It really put me on the map in a way, though of course, I don't just want to be remembered for the Christina Aguilera scandal. What it showed me was, even though I've only been on the commercial market for seven or eight months, I've really burned graphic images of my visuals onto the irises of my fans. They saw a huge, Grammy-winning star, who's been around for years, and they recognized Lady Gaga. That to me is quite an accomplishment."

She was spot on, but even here, she was careful to keep everyone on side. Unlike Amy Winehouse, who spent much of her early years of stardom criticizing everyone she could think of, Lady Gaga was playing a totally different game: "I think she's wonderful and no enemies here," she continued. "Most of the comparisons people say is 'your look' is the same, but this isn't my 'look,' this is my life. I dress like this all the time, you're not gonna ever catch me at the grocery store in flip-flops." Indeed.

On August 19, 2008, Lady Gaga's first album, *The Fame*, was released in the US. Over the next few months, it premiered pretty much across the world. The strategy behind it had been brilliant, of course: a combination of two sensational singles and even more amazing accompanying videos prepared the ground for the new release, on top of which there was Lady Gaga herself.

She was a marketing man's dream: extravagant in appearance, highly outspoken in her views, not afraid to talk about sex in all its various permutations, hinting at bisexuality, writing lyrics about disco sticks. And to cap it all, she had genuine talent, a formal musical training, an extremely astute grasp of modern celebrity and a considerable intellect that kept making itself felt, however much she might put herself forward as a frothy, bubblegum pop princess.

If ever an album was appropriately named, it was *The Fame*: so post-modernly ironic as to have worked her way through irony and back again, Lady Gaga was both embracing fame and laughing at herself and the world for doing so. Showing the kind of ambition that would propel her to the very top, she had worked for this moment, and for what it's worth, had achieved it at a younger age than Madonna, who was twenty-five when her first album, *Madonna*, came out in 1983. Lady Gaga was just twenty-two.

The subject of *The Fame* was, of course, fame.

Two and a half years in the making, for Lady Gaga had started working on the material that would eventually be released while she was still part of the New York club scene; she not only wrote the lyrics, but worked in conjunction with RedOne on the album's melodies and synth work. "*The Fame* is about how anyone can feel famous," she explained. "Pop culture is art. It doesn't make you cool to hate pop culture, so I embraced it and you hear it all over *The Fame*. But it's a sharable fame: I want to invite you all to the party, I want people to feel a part of this lifestyle."

The Fame was both utterly of the moment and also a nod back to the glam rock she so adored. Alongside "Just Dance" and "Poker Face" was "LoveGame" (featuring the disco stick), "Paparazzi" (questioning whether fame and love can co-exist), "Boys Boys Boys" (an homage to Motley Crue's "Girls, Girls, Girls"), "Beautiful, Dirty, Rich" (about her time as a druggie), "Eh, Eh (Nothing Else I Can Say)" (a relationship break-up) and "Brown Eyes," inspired by Queen. And on top of that came "I Like It Rough," "Starstruck," "The Fame," "Money Honey," "Paper Gangsta" and "Summerboy."

She was also keen to draw out the importance of performance art as part of the album. "I just feel like this record is really different—you've got everything from club bangers to more seventies glam, to more singer-songwriter records to rock music," she said.

"*The Fame* is not about who you are—it's about how everybody wants to know who you are! Buy it and listen to it before you go out, or in the car. I think you've really got to allow artists' creativity to marinate.

"It took me a while, but really delving into myself, I finally got it. I couldn't be more proud of it. It's not just a record—it's a whole pop art movement. It's not just about one song."

Indeed, at times she was bursting with so much pride that she sounded more like an excited teenager than a woman on the verge of international stardom. For all that she felt it had taken her a while to make her breakthrough, she was still, after all, very young and even the most jaded would have been thrilled by what had been happening over the past few months. Indeed, Lady Gaga just could not contain herself: "This idea of *The Fame* runs through and through," she continued. "Basically, if you have nothing—no money, no fame, you can still feel beautiful and dirty rich. It's about making choices, and having references—things you pull from your life that you believe in. It's about self-discovery and being creative. The record is slightly focused, but it's also eclectic. The music is intended to inspire people to feel a certain way about themselves so they'll be able to encompass in their own lives a sense of inner fame that they can project to the world and the carefree nature of the album is a reflection of that aura. I like to funnel interesting ideas to the rest of the world through a pop lens."

And the critics liked her latest work just as much as they had enjoyed the singles. "*The Fame* arrives, packing an immensely addictive melody or an inescapable hook; virtually everything sounds like another hit single. *The Fame* certainly sounds like it could be big," predicted Alexis Petridis in the *Guardian*. "Fueled by heavy dance tracks and popping electronic beats, *The Fame* is a well-crafted sampling of feisty anti-pop in high quality," said Matthew Chisling from Allmusic. "Lady Gaga pulls out all the stops on *The Fame*, injecting hard-hitting synthesizers and crashing slicks and grooves. From its opening track until it closes, *The Fame* fails to come up short on funky sounds to amuse fans of this dance genre."

"*The Fame* is remarkably (and exhaustingly) pure in its vision of a world in which nothing trumps being beautiful, dirty, and rich," observed Mikael Wood of *Entertainment Weekly*. "In this economy, though, her high-times escapism has its charms."

In Britain, the album went down particularly well. "For a debut which celebrates posing, it's appropriate that you can judge this LP, from New York's self-styled pop icon Lady Gaga, by its cover," wrote Peter Robinson in *Observer Music Monthly*. "This is a superstylized electronic R&B album about boys, cars, money and fame. The songs have titles such as 'Beautiful, Dirty,

Rich' and 'Paparazzi.' It's all rather high-concept, but this Rihanna versus Fischerspooner experiment pays off: the tunes are massive."

"At first blush, Lady Gaga's frothy disco confections could easily be mistaken for the mindless booty bait dangled by, say, the Pussycat Dolls," said Sarah Rodman from the *Boston Globe*, in probably the most perceptive review. "But listen a little closer to the sly, snarky lyrics and glam grooves on this feisty debut and you'll hear that this former downtown New York spice girl has at least a few things on her dirty mind."

But not everyone was so enthusiastic: some felt that the subject matter was too shallow, while others considered the very sharp production made up for occasionally patchy quality. All the while, there could be no doubt that a major new talent had been launched.

The public's reaction, on the other hand, was incredibly and universally positive. The album reached number four on the Billboard 200 and number one on the Billboard Top Electronic Albums chart, where it stayed for forty non-consecutive weeks. Worldwide, it sold eight million copies, reaching number one in a raft of countries, including the UK, while Lady Gaga appeared on numerous television programs including *So You Think You Can Dance*, *The Tonight Show With Jay Leno*, Ireland's *Tubridy Tonight*, the 57th Miss Universe contest in Vietnam, and so on. Some tracks from the album were featured in the TV series *Gossip*

Girl and in the New Year (of more later), Lady Gaga appeared on *American Idol*. In all, it was quite a debut.

And people were beginning to learn that to underestimate her would be at their peril. Writing in the *Daily Mail*, Adrian Thrills made the point that here was no young bimbo: "With her bleached blonde hair, hot pants and a stage show that involves sequins, disco lights and mirror balls, Gaga, twenty-two, certainly has the looks and style," he commented. "But she is also her own woman and, in reality, lies closer to a young Madonna or Cyndi Lauper. She has written songs for the Pussycat Dolls, Britney Spears and New Kids On The Block, and is now set to take center stage herself."

She'd done it; she'd cracked it, and at the tender age of twenty-two, Lady Gaga, née Stefani Germanotta, was a bona fide star. But that was just the first step. In order to have a long-term career, she must prove that this was no flash in the pan, that she was able to build on the success of the first album and the singles to date. Before she had been a complete unknown, now there was everything to play for. Would Lady Gaga be able to do it? Could she follow up this remarkable year?

Lady Gaga pretty-in-pink for the 2009 Brit Awards at Earls Court in London.

Above left: Lady Gaga takes time out to pose with one of her fans.

Above right: Out and about in Paris.

Below left: 'Papping' the paparazzi – Lady Gaga on the other side of the lens.

Above: She's on fire! In concert at Club Zapata in Germany.

Below: Forever blowing bubbles... Lady Gaga rocked a similar look (though with fewer bubbles) on the cover of *Rolling Stone* magazine's annual Hot List.

Lady Gaga was the opening act for The Pussycat Dolls (*above*) during their World Domination Tour – and many claimed she stole the show.

Opposite: Lady Gaga's concerts are always larger than life and a grand spectacle for her fans.

Lady Gaga performing at Glastonbury during the summer of 2009. Her shiny disco-ball inspired outfit and piano guitar wowed the crowd.

Not always such a fan of the paparazzi, Lady Gaga tries to scare the photographers off with vampire-fangs.

CHAPTER 5

LOVE AND
SUCCESS

ANUARY 2009, AND LADY GAGA WAS
making headlines all over the world:
there hadn't been such a spectacular
debut in decades. Her singles and CD
were all selling well; her live performances were incredibly popular and bringing the house down while she
herself was loving every minute of it. So too was the
media. This convent-educated, formally trained singer-
turned-bad-girl was a gift from showbiz heaven and the
more people saw her, the more they wanted a part of
her. And Lady Gaga was more than happy to oblige.

It was the Italian-Catholic background that particularly appealed. There was the Madonna precedent,
of course, but Italian-American girls weren't supposed
to behave like this. They were meant to stay home,
cook pasta and talk about the old country, not tour the
country in increasingly outlandish costumes that left
little to the imagination, talking about disco sticks. She

might have cooked meatballs for her boyfriend wearing just her knickers in the past, but Lady Gaga certainly had no time for such pastimes now. There was a whole world out there to conquer and she was getting on with it in her own unique way.

Her parents had accepted her success, though, and so, it turned out, had her grandparents. She was asked what they thought of it all: "They approve," she said. "My grandmother is basically blind, but she can make out the lighter parts, like my skin and hair. She says, 'I can see you, because you have no pants on.' So I'll continue to wear no pants, even on television, so that my grandma can see me."

Just how can anyone criticize a character who comes out with lines like that? Of course, there would always be a conservative element who fretted about what they saw as her decadence, but Lady Gaga was so blatant, so utterly unconcerned about it, there was nothing they could do. If they accused her of blatant nudity, she agreed; if they expressed concerns about her bisexuality, she was untroubled. As long as her records continued to sell—which they were doing, massively—who cared?

Success attracts attention, as Lady Gaga was finding out now. She had never had the slightest problem in attracting men, but now they flocked to her, something she quickly dismissed. "I don't give them a chance to even try a chat-up line," she declared. "I give them a firm, 'No!' before they even speak. That does the trick: you can't have love and success, but that doesn't bother me—I don't want love." In actual fact, someone was already lurking in the background, but she had a point. It might have been more accurate, though, to say that you can't have domesticity and success—and there was certainly no chance of her opting for that.

Not everyone loved her, though. Some of her fellow celebrities took a rather more cautious view: "I don't get her," said lead vocalist and bass guitarist Tyson Ritter of the All-American Rejects. "I don't think the song or the concept is as cool as people say it is. She's supposed to be this high-fashion person, but I don't think the music fits—it's not particularly edgy."

Someone else who was less than enthusiastic was Gabriella Cilmi, Australian singer and songwriter, best-known for her debut single, "Sweet About Me:" "Eventually you're just going to catch something and have to go to hospital, if you keep walking around in your bra and knickers," she wryly observed, but a substantial chunk of the rest of the world just didn't agree with her.

With the onset of the New Year, Lady Gaga turned her efforts into really whipping up a media storm about her, with stunning success. She had been touring with the Pussycat Dolls and credited them with her enjoyment at seeing women cavort about in their panties: "I love a girl in her underwear," she stated happily. "I've been writing for PCD, so Nicole Scherzinger has been in my head. There's something that's very humbling about being able to write for a powerhouse group like that."

But of course, this actually dated back to her schooldays. "I used to get in trouble a lot for wearing very low-cut shirts and see-through stuff with bras," she went on, as the media lapped it up. "We were definitely bad kids in a good environment. I mean, I was actually a very good student. I just sort of stuck out like a sore thumb—no different than today."

Meanwhile, the comparisons with Madonna continued, and Lady Gaga herself could see why the two artists were so often spoken of in the same breath: "We have a lot in common—the Lower East Side thing, I'm Italian, I was a brunette and I went blonde . . . I'm very exhibitionist," she confirmed. "But I also think I bring something new."

She certainly did that. In January, "Just Dance" hit the number-one slot, becoming notable in Britain for the fact that it knocked *X-Factor* 2008 winner Alexandra Burke from the top of the charts. Lady Gaga was usually pretty generous about her fellow celebrities, but she couldn't resist a sharp remark here: "I'm no TV talent show wannabe," she said. "I did this the way you are supposed to; I played every club in New York and found myself as an artist. I learned how to survive as an artist and how to fail, and then figure out who I was as a singer and performer. And I worked hard."

There were some naysayers in the press, however, calling Lady Gaga and various others not much more than Madonna wannabes, but the more perceptive among them spotted a new trend going on. A couple of other female artists—Little Boots and La Roux—were emerging at the same time. Also the real deal as opposed to manufactured talent-show acts, industry observers were predicting that the three of them represented the future. "The time is really right for this new breed of pop stars and I think what's interesting with them, as opposed to some of the more manufactured ones, is that they have much more of a DIY ethic," observed Krissi Murison, then deputy editor of *NME*. "I think they've got long careers in front of them as opposed to being one-hit wonders."

Lady Gaga was in Britain now, the first of a number of visits she would pay that year. Her unique clothes sense most certainly hadn't deserted her: that month she was photographed walking around in a green leotard and not a lot more. Then she was pictured in sparkly pants, a flesh-colored top and fishnets, and to cap it all off, there was the PVC corset, fishnets and open-toed sandals on a music television show. But it was all part of the role: fashion was as integral to her work as the music, something she was eager to explain.

"I've got to try to keep my figure down," she insisted. "I have these amazing fashion outfits, but they're very intricate or graphic, and pretty uncomfortable sometimes, depending on what train wreck of an idea I've got in my head. I need people to have a memory of what it feels like to hear me on the radio, to know what my videos look like. They're acquainted with my fashion, then they go to the show and it all comes together.

"I'm empowered by fashion, and my work. What I do is performance art—it's pop music meant for the Louvre. I write about sequins, parties and fame; and how I wish modern America was more like the Andy Warhol era. If you say something long enough, people will listen. Warhol kept telling people, 'This is art, this is art, this is art,' and eventually they said, 'Andy Warhol is brilliant, he is the future of art.' You just have to keep hammering the image."

She loved clothes, too. In London, she was spotted spending almost $8,000 in the boutique Lipsy, splashing out on a basque, Lycra and denim garments. "She wants to get everyone horny as hell," said her friend, Canadian rapper Kardinal Offishall. "She doesn't care what anyone else thinks of her walking through the cold streets of London in a bra and her panties." And even when she was pictured in something more conventional, she managed a wild and wacky hairdo: the object was to keep the punter guessing, and she did.

The Paris Hilton connection was also providing the public with a good deal of fun. Some people, probably inaccurately, saw Paris as the inspiration behind *The Fame*, with her clear message about "how anyone can feel famous." The bloggers were all having their say: "Lady Gaga is clearly talking about the do-nothing heir-head she went to school with," observed one. "There's no doubt she's poking fun at Paris," said another.

In actual fact, she was making a more general comment about the nature of fame, but the association provided such amusement that people simply could not resist speculating. A friend of Paris downplayed the connection: "They barely knew each other at school, other than perhaps nodding as they passed in the corridor."

But Lady Gaga was making a very observant point about the differing nature of fame. "I think there's different kinds of fame," she said. "I think there's 'fame,' which is plastic and you can buy it on the street, and paparazzi and money and being rich, and then there's 'the fame,' which is when no one knows who you are, but everybody wants to know who you are."

Indeed, the Lady herself felt that everyone could aspire to the latter: "That's what this whole record's about, this record beckons for everybody on the planet to stop being either jealous or obsessive about what they don't have and start acting like they do," she continued. "It's carrying yourself down the street like, 'I'm beautiful and dirty rich, but I've got no money.' Fame is not pretending to be rich, it's carrying yourself in a way that exudes confidence and passion for music or art or fishing, or whatever the hell it is that you're passionate about, and projecting yourself in a way that people say, 'Who the fuck is that?'

"It has nothing to do with money. I can wear a two-dollar pair of pants and a T-shirt and a pair of sunglasses for two bucks on the street, but I can make it look like I'm Paris Hilton. You gotta have the fame, you gotta exude that thing. You gotta make people care, you gotta know and believe how important you are. You gotta have conviction in your ideas." That statement actually ended up as a compliment to Paris, implying that she too was a someone, but still the online debate raged, all the same.

Lady Gaga was certainly making a splash. The Pussycat Dolls' Doll Domination Tour got underway in January 2009 with Gaga as their warm-up: by this time she was attracting almost as much attention as the headlining act. And the media were really sitting up and taking notice now, not just putting her outlandish outfits on the front pages and posting blogs about her on websites, but talking to her seriously about her art.

Lady Gaga explained to one interviewer that she was making use of small, home-shot videos: "I just shot these films called *crevettes*," she said. "That's what I call them: it means shrimps, in French. And shrimps are small, but decadent and tasty, which is how I think my films should be." Clearly, she was the real deal: she wasn't putting it on. Here was a highly intelligent and educated young woman who was in charge of the various strands of her career, and who could even come up with cultural references in other languages, as well.

Indeed, Lady Gaga continued to find the UK an increasingly positive experience. Because she was so very controversial, as was her music, it had been hard to make the initial breakthrough in the US, whereas in Britain they were lapping her up. "We've been trying to get it ['Just Dance'] played in the US since March," she admitted, and while they succeeded eventually, it had been far more of a battle to gain airtime there than it proved to be in the UK. "I mean, it just doesn't sound like Katy Perry's 'I Kissed A Girl'—which is a beautiful, lovely, amazing hit record and it sounds like a radio hit. My song doesn't sound like a radio hit. I mean, it does, but it doesn't. Now here, in the UK, it might, because electro-pop is not this stinky underground thing, it's a real genre. But in America, electro-pop is dirty under-ground music."

Of course, what she was really producing was dance music and that went down far better in the UK. "I am taking it to another level," she continued. "I mean, my records are borderline dance records. They've got a real electro-rock heart and soul, and the vibe of the sentiment is pop, but there's a lot of people that were like, 'This is a dance record.'"

So she got out there. "I played show after show after show, and murdered every single one of them," she conceded. "In the arena I'd look at everybody and go, 'Some of you know this song and me, and some of you don't, but you're sure as hell gonna know who the hell I am before I leave this arena tonight!' And then I would sing my record. And it's just relentless and fearless, and I'm gonna fucking make my mark this year, right now. I just really, really have been the kind of person that's unstoppable and I've never let anything get in my way."

The sheer force of her personality was now becoming clear. Like so many of the most successful women in show business, she was turning into the star that she wanted to be, not through using her beauty, but by transforming herself into a beautiful woman. It is not disparaging to say that Lady Gaga was not born with staggering good looks: pictures of her as a teenager and in the early years of her career show a perfectly attractive young woman, albeit one with a very individual dress sense, but no traffic-stopper. Now all that was beginning to change. By whatever means possible, she was turning into a stunning woman: lithe and sexy, with a beautiful face. In her determination to look the part, she was

succeeding without having been born into the traditional sexpot role, something she was well aware of
herself.

"I'm not super-sexy," she revealed in one interview, though if truth be told she was becoming that
way. "A girl's got to use what she's given and I'm not
going to make a guy drool the way a Britney video
does, so I take it to extremes. I don't say I dress sexily
on stage—what I do is so extreme. It's meant to make
guys think: 'I don't know if this is sexy or just weird.'
They start off thinking it's freaky, then realize it's sexy
because I'm having such a good time up there."

At this point, her stage costumes might not have
been overtly sexy as opposed to extravagant but they
were about to become so. By the time she made the
video for "Bad Romance," her garb was so overtly
provocative that no one could have been in any doubt
about the image she was presenting, and as for not
being Britney—no, she wasn't. But she didn't need to
be: not even Britney had ever cultivated the sort of
headlines Lady Gaga was garnering now.

But the fact was that she had well and truly
worked out how to use the system. "Let's be honest:
when the record company met me I was on stage at a
bar in a thong, setting hairspray on fire, singing songs
about oral sex," she told one interviewer. "I can sit here
and talk about art all day, but most of my fans are just
gonna be bopping around to that killer beat. But that's

not dumbing down: I have just become smarter about channelling my ideas through a pop lens."

Another aspect of Lady Gaga that makes her so unusual is the completeness of her image as a pop star. Britney Spears was Britney Spears on stage, but apart from her well-documented meltdown, away from the bright lights she was pretty much an all-American girl, with two cute little boys and a love of vacationing in hot spots. Even Madonna, despite her many transformations, was a noticeably different person on- and off-stage, stepping into whatever character she was assuming while performing, but still not unaccustomed to climbing into tracksuit bottoms during down time.

But Lady Gaga was Lady Gaga, wherever she was and whatever she was doing. Her entire life had become her act. Indeed, the only thing that worried her about that leotard shot was that by her standards, this was dressing down: "I am very into fashion—it's everything to me," she conceded. "When I'm writing music, I'm thinking about the clothes I want to wear on stage. The most I dress down in is a leotard—I was frustrated when the English paparazzi caught me dressed like that last week: it was as dowdy as I ever get. I'm not a T-shirt-and-jeans girl at all, not even at home on the couch."

In some ways, what she was beginning to resemble was the old-fashioned image of the Hollywood star.

By the Noughties, dressing down was very much the new dressing up: off-duty, the Hollywood A-list simply slouched about in jeans and tees, allowing themselves to look as grungy as possible as if in some perverse way to make the point that they were so gorgeous, they didn't need to bother to get washed or even comb their hair. And pop stars were even worse.

But Lady Gaga seemed to point back to an era where glamor was everything, for when she wasn't in one of her more eccentric outfits she appeared groomed within an inch of her life. To be a star, you have to dress like a star, she seemed to be saying, and why not? Old-era Hollywood understood that if they wanted the public to make them rich by going out to see their movies, then the least they could do was to maintain some standards in return. Lady Gaga understood that if she wanted people to treat her as the consummate professional star, then she would have to look the part, on- and off-stage. Her great hero Andy Warhol turned his entire life into an artwork and she was determined to do just the same.

Of course, there was the minor matter that despite provoking headlines almost every time she walked down the street, Lady Gaga was still the supporting act for the Pussycat Dolls' current tour. She was garnering far more attention than the girls themselves, but if they themselves cared, they were too smart to show it— "She's great, it's really cool," said one of the Pussycats,

Melody Thornton. The band was earning a great deal of acclaim for their act, but even so Lady Gaga was winning the publicity battle, hands down.

Indeed, everyone she worked with was being generous about her, including Donnie Wahlberg of New Kids On The Block, with whom she had also toured: "Lady Gaga is delicious—we got quite close," he said. "We co-wrote a song, she's very talented. I didn't have sex with her, but I wouldn't say no."

And an increasing number of men agreed.

Although "Just Dance" was released in the States almost a year earlier, it was only now that it was apparent quite how successful it had become. For Lady Gaga a whole new chapter in her life had opened up and she was loving every minute. There was even the sense that she wouldn't be a supporting act for much longer, although she herself was far too tactful to come right out with it, but she was utterly thrilled with the success she was now enjoying.

"It's subliminal," she told one interviewer. "I've got every person on the planet in a club somewhere saying, 'I love this record baby' [a line from the song]. Success is built in! To me there is nothing more powerful than one song that you can put on in a room anywhere in the world and somebody gets up and dances. That's what pop is, it resonates on a visceral level. If you put a classical piece on, it may resonate intellectually, but everyone's not gonna get up and mobilize."

True enough, although it occasionally sounded as if Lady Gaga was justifying herself for going into pop music rather than classical. "I may not be Beethoven, but if you want a sick synth line, I'm your girl," she declared. But the fact was that she wanted to appeal to the masses, something she would never do had she become a classical pianist, as once seemed possible. On the other hand, there's pop and then there's pop. Lady Gaga's pop was clever, witty and intelligent. In an age that could bestow instant fame, she questioned the very nature of what it was to be famous. And though she was still young, it was true: she had done it the traditional way; she'd worked incredibly hard for what she'd achieved and there was no sign of letting up.

Even so, the extent of her success seemed to astonish even her. Her fame was global, even if it was Britain in particular that seemed to "get" her act; Lady Gaga had come to personify that old show-business cliché about working for years to become an overnight success. And there had been stages along the way, as well. She had, after all, achieved some fame (or perhaps notoriety) on the underground New York club scene, an early manifestation of what was to come—even so, she had never expected this. But having got to where she was now, in January 2009 she found herself becoming more ambitious still.

"I guess success is only as big or small as you see it," she told one interviewer. "I thought I was quite successful two years ago, and I think I'm quite successful now but I've got a long way to go. It's funny, I was sitting in the car and my manager's reading me off all the stats and the things that are happening, and he's like, 'This is great, Gaga!' And I'm like, 'I know, but for some reason I feel like we've accomplished nothing and we've got so far to go.' And he's like, 'You're on the same page as me.' You know what I mean? Because I don't wanna be one song: I wanna be the next twenty-five years of pop music, but it's really hard to measure that kind of ambition."

It has been said that the really successful people never really feel as if they're successful because once they've conquered one peak, they immediately start looking for the next, and it was increasingly clear that Lady Gaga fitted that same mold. A few years previously, she would never have dreamed of the kind of success she was experiencing now, and yet far from sitting back and luxuriating in it, as some pop stars did (to their cost—they didn't remain so for long), she was fretting about the future. The pop industry is a notoriously difficult one in which to maintain a long-term career, especially for women, but that was what she was aiming for now. There had been some women who'd managed it, and Lady Gaga was determined to be one of them, too.

"That kind of blonde ambition is looked at with a raised brow because most artists don't have longevity today, especially in fun music that's about underwear and pornography and money," she said rather perceptively. "[But there's] Madonna, Britney's been around for a long time, Grace Jones is unstoppable, David Bowie was around for years and years, The Beatles. . . .

"I strive to be a female Warhol. I want to make films and music, do photography and paint one day, maybe. Make fashion. Make big museum art installations. I would be a bit more mixed-media than him, probably—combining mixed media and imagery, and doing more of a kind of a weird pop-art piece." High ambition, indeed.

Meanwhile, she certainly knew how to keep the cameras popping. In Birmingham, she appeared on stage in ripped tights (prompting much good-humored jesting about what the Pussycats' claws might have done to her), and then went one better by announcing that she could have been a Doll herself. "I was writing tracks for them at the time, but I had my vibe and my own style," she observed. "Their style is not mine, fashion-wise—it wasn't right for me." It was a wise decision: she was now totally eclipsing the Dolls, who remained incredibly gracious about it all, and it was clear that soon she would be headlining a tour of her own.

She was certainly more in demand than ever: she

was asked to act as DJ at the launch of Nokia 5800 in London before doing likewise, clad in bra, PVC skirt and shades, with Mark Ronson at London's Maya nightclub. Meanwhile, men continued to drool, although she was as uncompromising about this as everything else: "If a guy is intimidated by me, then he can fuck off!" she told one interviewer. "I don't want to waste my time on a man who doesn't like smart women. My dream man would have to be smarter than me—sadly, I think there's one or two men out there who qualify. Sean Connery as James Bond, that's a real man." Talk of finding a real *woman*, meanwhile, had begun to taper off.

It was Lily Allen who, with "The Fear," managed to knock her off the number one slot in February 2009, but it really didn't matter anymore. "Poker Face" was about to come out in the UK, and Lady Gaga continued to shock, while thoroughly enjoying herself. She was asked her advice for Valentine's Day, a red rag to a bull if ever there was one: "Watch your lipstick at the dinner table, because if you wear a red lipstick or a good thick lipstick and you've got your napkin, it looks really messy and you get it all over your face," she said. "Maybe wear something lighter . . . but guys like a good wet mouth." Of course, it made the papers—again.

Indeed, as the love affair with Britain continued, she lost no opportunity to praise the country, while at the same time delivering statements that made the press. When the tour reached Liverpool, she was on good form: "Liverpool is really the birth of the sexual revolution for women, with the birth of The Beatles," she said, somewhat inexplicably. "Without them, I don't think that women would be taking their cardigans off in hallways. I'm pleased to see that it's mostly women who are dominating the charts. America thinks I'm strange; they like my music, but they think I'm very strange. I couldn't care less. What's so powerful about being in the UK is that there's such an open and free spirit about pop music. Over the next twenty-five years I intend to prove that I am an artist and not just a celebrity who dresses well. Pop music historically produces joy, which we all could use right now during this terrible recession."

It was vintage Gaga, delivered with aplomb.

In Ireland, meanwhile, Lady Gaga became the first artist since Madonna (natch) in 1985 to reach numbers one and two in the charts, with "Just Dance" and "Poker Face." (Madonna's contributions had been "Into The Groove" and "Holiday.")

Back in Britain, she performed at the Brit Awards in February, going down like crazy with her fellow musicians and the public alike. She sang with the Pet Shop Boys, who were there to receive an Outstanding Contribution to Music award, and yet she managed to outshine everyone else there. (There was, incidentally, a tanning booth backstage, of which she made extravagant use.) It was generally agreed that she managed to upstage everyone else present, even the Killers' Brandon Flowers: she was dressed in a sort of two-piece bikini with matching headdress that looked as if it was made of porcelain.

Needless to say, her latest look garnered acres of media coverage, along with the catty observation that all she needed was a few flowers and she'd look like a vase. Then there was a quick change into a very revealing pink dress for the after party, when Lady Gaga again managed to upstage everyone else, including the whole of Girls Aloud.

And the love affair with Britain continued. "I adore being in the UK, but the shows that I've done so far, with Pussycat Dolls and on my own, are nothing to what you will see from me," she told one journalist. "The dollar is so bad I haven't been able to take over all my equipment and do a full set—but I will. The US don't get me like you guys do, but it doesn't bother me. I have my own tour planned across the States in March then I'll be back to see you guys in April.

"I'm not interested in settling down: I just want to make music and fuck random people. I want to be around for twenty-five years. I admire Madonna and Courtney Love, and the way they re-invent themselves and kick ass—I want to do that and be even bigger."

She was going about it in the right way. Clothing continued to appear to be an optional extra: Lady Gaga was photographed at the Universal Records' after-party with her nipples clearly on display. The event was at the esteemed Claridges, not the most obvious venue for nipple flashing, but then Lady Gaga was rewriting the rulebook as she went along. Next stop was Paris, where she wasn't actually naked, but looked it, wearing a skin-colored leotard and jacket. Naturally, the pictures appeared everywhere—just as the Lady and her entourage hoped they would.

GOING GLOBALLY GAGA

ESPITE THE FACT THAT SHE WAS RELATIVELY new on the international music scene, such was Lady Gaga's impact that major established artists now clamored to work with her. The Swedish singer September was one: she was delighted when Gaga recorded a version of her song "Sin Of My Own." Hugh Hefner was another fan: he invited the diva to pose nude for *Playboy*.

Some people were stunned when she turned his offer down, given her laissez-faire attitude towards clothing (really, sometimes it was just not necessary at all), but to seasoned Gaga-watchers, her decision was no surprise. She was taking the world on on her own terms, not on those of men like Hefner, although she was canny enough to remark, "I might change my mind when I have a new album to plug." Chances are she wouldn't, though—Lady Gaga was proving to be more than adept at drumming up publicity on her own.

But she didn't talk trash about Hefner—indeed, with few notable exceptions she never criticized anyone, wisely acknowledging that in a business like the one she was in, you need all the friends you can get. Besides, posing in *Playboy* has been a comeback option for many a performer in the past and there was no point in ruling anything out.

Katy Perry was another on the list: the two met up in Marseilles, where Lady Gaga gave the "I Kissed A Girl" singer French lessons. "I told Katy to say, '*Ça va, Marseilles?*'—which means, 'How you doing?'" she related. "Because I guarantee they will go nuts, if you say it." Nor was that all—Lady Gaga asked for a kiss— "It was so I could say, 'I kissed a girl.'" Indeed, she'd already made more than enough hints, but Lady Gaga was not one to miss an opportunity.

Then, in one of the more spectacular meetings of egos in the year, she was pictured out partying with Paris Hilton—*that* Paris Hilton. Clearly the two had decided that it was far more advantageous to exploit their connection than feud about it, and so they posed together at the Nokia 5800 launch, Paris's studiedly mini-skirted look set against Lady Gaga's hair, which had been styled into a neat bow.

Gary Go was another. The pop-rock singer ("Wonderful") and supporting act for Take That performed with Lady Gaga in London, where they had a slightly unconventional meeting: "I did a cover of Lady

Gaga's track 'Just Dance' recently," he revealed. "I chose it because I was thinking about her quite a lot. We met when we both played London's Koko venue this year. She was in the dressing room opposite me and someone shouted to her to come and meet Gary Go. She shouted back that she had no clothes on, but two seconds later she just came to the door with nothing on, then quickly threw a little jacket on.

"It was quite a meeting and she is very attractive. She's a performance artist, so I guess she doesn't have any inhibitions, but it certainly had an effect on me. And, yes, I am single, and G G and Gaga—well, I guess it does have a ring to it." Lady Gaga didn't take him up on his offer, but then nor did she decline it. The only enemies she was making were other stars who found her too over-the-top or were jealous of her success. Of course, the smart ones in the latter camp simply shut up.

And Gary Go was right: she was a performance artist, after all, and simply couldn't stop herself from wanting to shock. Meanwhile, her outfits grew more garish by the day: another one had her typically in hot pants, bra, open leather jacket, sunglasses, an elegant black straw hat and thigh-high white boots with black laces. Oh, and she was carrying a parasol and only the central part of her mouth was painted in black lipstick.

Freed from the constraints of writing for other performers, Lady Gaga was not only enjoying playing with her appearance, but also taking the music much further than she could have done previously. Her lyrics are far more explicit than those sung by most female pop stars—it's just not possible to contemplate Britney Spears singing some of the words that Lady Gaga was now mouthing with such relish. Those songs were not of middle America; rather they were dark, often threatening and very much from the fetish-ridden New York club scene, where Lady Gaga had learned her trade. It was hardly surprising that she'd had problems making her breakthrough—what was incredible was that she was now being allowed to get away with so much.

"Sometimes when I do something for myself, I'll be a little bit more risk-taking," she admitted. "I'll just think about something that I could maybe handle that nobody else could, but I pretty much approach them the same way. Writing a pop song and a big chorus, it's like it's kind of just special for each song. And sometimes I'll tailor-make something for a particular artist and use them as my muse, but in terms of melody and stuff, I always sort of come from the same soul place."

As well as avoiding making enemies for herself, she was enthusiastic in her praise of her colleagues. Clearly, she had found exactly the right team to bring out the best in her and she knew it, too. She was sensible enough to realize that she would not have been able to get so far on her own, and that Akon and RedOne were of paramount importance to her success.

"Akon is a very talented songwriter to work with," she said. "His melodies, they're just insane. It's funny, I think about him a lot when I'm doing my melodies because he's so simple, and he's just been great. He keeps me on my feet, very grounded, but he also puts me on a silver platter which is always very nice. So it's been an incredible influence. It's like every time you work with somebody that's better than you are, you become greater."

It is a rare pop star, especially one who has achieved the kind of success that Lady Gaga was enjoying, who is able to praise another artist for having a greater talent, but alongside all the bravado, there has always been a curiously modest aspect to her. It is one of the qualities that has helped her to succeed. While she might have been capable of taking a firm stance with her record company about the kind of music she wanted to produce, at the same time she was able to see that she would do so much better if she took the advice of others in the industry. And not only was Akon able to guide her in the right direction, he could keep her grounded, too. Sudden success, especially on this scale, can turn heads and ruin an artist in the process: it was imperative at this stage that Lady Gaga had someone to help her deal with it all.

She was even more enthusiastic about RedOne. "RedOne is like the heart and soul of my universe," she admitted. "I met him and he completely, one hundred and fifty thousand percent wrapped his arms around my talent, and it was like we needed to work together. He has been a pioneer for the Haus of Gaga and his influence on me has been tremendous; I really couldn't have done it without him. He taught me in his own way—even though he's not a writer, he's a producer— he taught me how to be a better writer, because I start- ed to think about melodies in a different way." And that affection was more than reciprocated and he, too, helped her stay on track. With such a buzz of creativ- ity surrounding her, it was hardly surprising that she was going from strength to strength.

Along with much else, fame brings with it some surprises, though, no matter how well-planned the debut, how down-to-earth the artist (which Lady Gaga was in many ways). She was getting accustomed to other stars taking note of her outfits, especially those that stole the front pages, and wearing something simi- lar soon afterwards, but what came as more of a shock was a tribute from a very young child. Lady Gaga's sub- ject matter was adult-oriented, to put it mildly, but she was creating very catchy music and so it was inevitable that the younger generation would listen in—and then try to do it for themselves. A video was posted online of a young girl singing Lady Gaga's songs, and the Lady herself was more than a little taken aback.

"I'm not sure how I feel about a six-year-old danc- ing to a song about being wasted, but she's so cute, it doesn't matter," is what she said. But she was discovering something else: frequently, when you become famous (and whether you want it or not), you also become a role model. In many ways, she was an excellent figurehead for older girls: someone who went after what she wanted and let nothing stand in her way—but younger girls? It was probably best if they didn't go too far in copying Lady Gaga's look—not that there was a lot she could do about it. Fame is not always easy, even when you're capable of singing about it in a post-modern ironic way.

On the upside, her work had now become so ubiquitous that it was everywhere, so much so that Lady Gaga herself wasn't always sure when she was about to hear it. Her music especially was frequently played on American TV, and not just *Gossip Girl*, often taking its creator by surprise. She herself was thrilled. "That happens all the time and I call the record label and I'm like, 'I didn't know that song was on that show,'" she admitted. "There have been so many licenses recently that I don't even hear about all of them. But that makes me feel great because it tells me that my goal, which was to analyze and reckon and struggle with ideas about pop culture, it's really working because all of these shows that are so emblematic of modern television and modern film and modern movies and modern club shows, it's like they're all gravitating towards my stuff, because I guess it's speaking to something that's very today."

And she now started to become the recipient of another, very different type of flattery—others began to satirize her on TV shows, always a sure sign that someone has arrived. Jay Leno had already done so in the States and now it was the turn of the UK. In January 2009, the comedienne Catherine Tate appeared on Channel 4's *The Sunday Night Project* with Alan Carr and Justin Lee Collins: all three sported peroxide bobs, pretending to be Lady Gaga. Collins, naturally, still had a beard.

It was all good-natured fun and a sign of how popular Lady Gaga had become. In March, much to everyone's regret, she returned to LA, but with the promise of returning soon for her own headline tour. And she kept herself in the news with no effort at all: she was warned again, by the police, that her propensity to leave the house wearing only PVC and a jacket could get her in trouble: "It's not that I don't like pants, I just choose not to wear them some days," she protested. "I think no pants is sexy, I love the naked human body. I was working in strip clubs when I was eighteen."

She had now coined a new phrase to describe her style—retrosexual. "I came out with that a long time ago," she explained to one interviewer. "Me and my buddy Tom were hanging out one day in the studio and we were talking about metrosexuals because he had bought a pair of boots and I said, 'Those are very metrosexual.' And he was like, 'I don't know, I think they're kind of retro.' And I said, 'So you're retrosexual.'"

"It was kind of a joke. The more I thought about it—I'm so obsessed with all things retro, the seventies and eighties—I don't know, that word just kind of flew out of my mouth one day and it stuck with me. I often do that: if I coin terms, they'll become like the center-fold of my entire project or an entire record."

It was indeed a perfect summary of the Gaga style although it wasn't just the seventies and eighties that formed so much of her work. There continued to be something quite visionary about it all: her style of dress could be incredibly futuristic (another costume had her in a gold corset and a headpiece that looked as if it represented the Milky Way) and then she was, of course, setting the agenda in a manner few pop stars are able to do. In some ways, she was a magpie, taking pieces out of individual cultures and using them to suit her needs. Her make-up often seemed based on Kabuki, the heavily-stylized Japanese theatrical tradition, her costumes like nothing before. And while in the early outings, she often sported a Bowie-esque lightning flash on her cheek, it appeared increasingly rarely these days. Now she was more her own woman than ever before.

And she had a way of describing it, too, saying that she "wrote music for the dress. I mean, I don't write records and then decide what the video will look like—I instantaneously write things at the same time so it's a complete vision, the song and the visual, the way that I would perform it on the stage. It's something that all comes to me at once. So when I say I make the music for the dress, the dress is a bit of a metaphor for 'I make the music for everything,' for the entire performance vision."

Although she was back in LA, the British fascination with Lady Gaga continued. It was announced that she would play various festivals in the UK that summer, something both she and the fans seemed to be looking forward to. "I can't wait for the festival season, especially muddy Glastonbury," she told the *Daily Star*. "I love all that. I play the Lollapalooza festival in America and actually, before anybody knew of me as an underground songwriter and pop musician, I was quite frequently naked and tripping on acid in fields with my friends."

Unsurprisingly, the media—and everyone else—loved it. For all that she was talking about nudity and drugs, there was something quite fresh and unforced about Lady Gaga, unlike most other pop stars. That same frankness sometimes came close to getting her in trouble: her record label, for a start, didn't like it at all but it was who she was, and to present herself in such a guileless way was really rather charming. She was certainly a one-of-a-kind.

Lady Gaga had previously spoken about preparing meatballs in her underwear: now that went on film. Shots emerged of a video she was making for the song "Eh Eh (Nothing Else I Can Say)," in which she was indeed in bra and panties, making meatballs in the kitchen. This was widely perceived as a nod to her Italian heritage, but it was just as likely to have been a reference to that long-lost love. For such a tough cookie, the experience had clearly made a huge impact on her—it continued to come up in interviews all the time.

Her newfound passion for all things English encompassed The Beatles and she couldn't help musing on what life might have been like, had she been around in their heyday. "I'm quite sure that if it were 1968, I may not be the Lady Gaga that I am today," she enthused. "I might be arguing with Yoko Ono and trying to win John Lennon's heart and chasing The Beatles in a bus on LSD, hoping that one of them hands me a microphone one day."

She certainly wasn't interested in winning anyone's heart at that stage, though: she remained a little coy about the great love in the past, but the effect of what had obviously been a traumatic break-up was merely to make her appreciate her career even more. "I've only ever really been in love once," she confided in one interviewer. "He didn't want me to do this job. He wanted me to stay at home, so I left. It broke my heart, but also made me realize music is my first love.

My music's never going to roll over in bed one morning and tell me it doesn't love me anymore: I have a problem with rejection."

It was a surprisingly vulnerable admission from a woman who gave a good impression of having a steely inner core. And she certainly proved capable of arousing strong emotions: the next to speak out was Alan Donohoe, lead singer with The Rakes. "I can't stand Lady Gaga," he declared. "She is basically selling crap to kids! I think she's terrible and really ugly, I hate her. Leona Lewis seems dull, but nice. She has standards, nice skin and can sing, whereas Lady Gaga is trash and dresses like a prostitute."

So what brought that on? Gaga herself could afford to laugh: the headlines were morphing into money in the bank and though cash may not have been her main motivator, it certainly didn't hurt. Back in the States, she was kicking off on another tour and while she had not completed her stint with the Pussycat Dolls worldwide, in this gig she was the headline act. Indeed, she now had a support act of her own: the retro-pop duo Chester French, whose guitarist Maxwell Drummey had recently distinguished himself with a brief marriage to Peaches Geldof. It wouldn't be long before she totally overtook the groups she had been supporting in the past.

That remark about music not rejecting her was also a telling one. At times, Lady Gaga's relationship with her muse did indeed seem almost a sexual one: on another occasion she commented, "It's really your job to have mind-blowing, irresponsible condomless sex with whatever idea it is you're writing about"—a remarkably apt image for her. She gave the impression that her entire life was like that: whatever she engaged with, she gave it her full attention, and that also applied to sex itself. Lady Gaga might not have had time for romance, but a little copulation wasn't out of the question—"I am the most sexually free woman on the planet," she said.

She certainly liked to tease. It wasn't just the clothes that revealed her exhibitionist tendency either: she wasn't above coming out with little snippets to entertain, too. "I had sex in the back of a taxi in New York," she told one interviewer. "It was fun—I'd do it again. It's always fun to do things that are sneaky. Sneaky sex is good. You know, sense memory is a powerful thing. I can give myself an orgasm just by thinking about it."

Ultimately, though, it was about the music. The more Lady Gaga performed, the more she wanted to do so: it became a great, virtuous circle in which the more famous she became, the more people wanted to see her and the more who saw her, the more her fame grew. That presented no problem at all to the Lady herself. She was now in a situation that most musicians would have given their right arms for, and she was revelling in

it, too. On the one hand, she might be said to be working too hard, but given how much she loved what she
did, it was hard to call it work. And very wisely, Lady
Gaga kept in touch with her roots, namely the club
scene. It was where she'd come from, and it was there
that she'd learned to judge what people liked: she
needed to keep a finger in that particular pie.

In what was becoming an increasingly booked-up
life, this was also a way of exercising spontaneity.
"Sometimes my tour manager and I will book shows
on the fly," she told one interviewer. "We'll say, 'Well,
we get off at nine tonight, why don't we see if the gay
club around the corner wants Lady Gaga to come?'
And they'll almost always say yes, and then we'll do a
show for free. I love to play and make music. It's funny
when you ask me about fame, because it's like I'm not
on the road right now working towards some ultimate
orgasmic explosion of fame that I have in [my] head."

Indeed, at times she could hardly contain her own
wonderment at the life she was leading. "I'm living my
dream right now," she admitted. "I'm on the road, I'm
making music, I'm making art, I'm performing at are-
nas and in nightclubs, and people know my lyrics. They
know my fashion and they know what I'm trying to
say, and it's affecting them. This is great, this is exactly
what I've always wanted."

But she knew the work couldn't let up. If she really wanted to fulfill her game plan of twenty-five years

at the top, not only would she have to work almost constantly, she would have to keep one step ahead of the pack. Innovation was everything. It was the only way Madonna managed to stay ahead and Lady Gaga knew that she must always be on the lookout for new ideas, themes, even people to work with, if she was really going to stay in front.

The ever-evolving look was all part of it. There had been rumors that she was about to launch her own range of clothing, but in reality she was content to stick with stylists such as Matthew Williams, her twenty-three-year-old creative director, who was known as Matty Dada and formed part of the Haus of Gaga. He was also an ex-boyfriend though work, as ever, took center stage: "Dada is quite brilliant and we were crazy lovers, but I stopped it when we discovered what a strong creative connection we had," she revealed. "I didn't want it just to be about careless love."

Williams was also the person who helped her discover the link between music, fashion and art. "My Jean-Paul Goude [another pet name for Matthew] was the inspiration that made the connection for me between the art world and the fashion world," she continued. "He used to say things like 'If you want to make a shoulder pad, don't research jackets—research sculpture, mineral rocks, paintings.' He thinks in a different way; he is the designer of the future."

And he wasn't the only one. Asked why she

hadn't yet brought out her own line, Lady Gaga replied, "Right now, I'm more concerned with using my fame to promote young designers such as Gary Card, an artist who designed a piece I used onstage. There hasn't been a commercial artist lately that has embodied avant-garde and couture so insistently as myself."

Unsurprisingly, given her love of all things fashion, she was also now frequently cited as a trendsetter herself. In the spring of 2009, there was a big fashion in sculpted hairstyles and no bigger devotee than Lady Gaga, who was seen out with her hair sculpted into a bow. Whether they admitted it or not, an increasing number of celebrities were copying the look, too, some more successfully than others.

She herself got away with some stratagems that others simply did not: it was perhaps a challenge to carry off flaxen hair and ruby-red lips, but somehow she managed it. The world was full of other females intent on aping this—and proving they could not. Indeed, even the Pussycat Dolls themselves seemed to take inspiration from Lady Gaga's wildness: in early 2009, they released a single "Whatcha Think About That" with an accompanying video harking back to their own burlesque roots. Dressed in provocative lingerie, they looked as if they'd carried away a few tricks from their supporting act. Onstage, they were becoming even more raunchy, too. Considering what they had to follow—another of Lady Gaga's costumes was hot pants and a metal breastplate—the stakes were getting higher, and so the girls started crotch grabbing with the rest of them. But somehow, night after night, Lady Gaga still managed to steal the show.

In March 2009, Lady Gaga took another massive step along her route to world domination. For the very first time she headlined her own tour, called "The Fame Ball," kicking off with a tour around the United States. Although Europe, especially the UK, completely adored her, it made sense for her to start on home turf, and while some of her fellow Americans might have considered her a little odd, others were thrilled by her. Shortly after tickets went on sale, more venues and more cities were added to the schedule. An amazing number of people wanted to see the new sensation headlining her own show.

Typically, she herself didn't see it so much as a concert tour, but more an extended piece of performance art. "It's not really a tour, it's more of a travelling party," she told *MTV News*. "I want it to be an entire experience from [the] minute you walk in [the] front door to [the] minute I begin to sing. And when it's all over, everyone's going to press rewind and relive it again. It's going to be as if you're walking into New York circa 1974: there's an art installation in the lobby, a DJ spinning your favorite records in the main room, and then the most haunting performance that you've ever seen on the stage.

"I'm on the phone every minute of every day, talking to people, being creative, planning this Ball, and my tour manager is constantly saying, 'Come on, we have to go, we've got to go right now!' But to me, the Ball is so important. I want so much to make every depression dollar that everyone spends on my show worth it. And yeah, I'm paying a lot for it—out of my own pocket. But that's OK, I just don't care about money."

Indeed, this was undoubtedly true—money had never been a motivating factor and at the time of writing, Lady Gaga hadn't so much as bought her own house. But she certainly cared about the performance. For a while now, she'd played second fiddle to a number of other groups and was clearly aching to get out there on her own: she'd served her time as an apprentice and now she was ready to step center-stage. This being Lady Gaga, three different versions of the show were prepared to cater for the different-sized venues she'd be playing, while she also added a charitable dimension by donating tickets to raise money for schools affected by budgetary cuts.

As usual, despite the too-cool-for-school act, Lady Gaga also came across like an excited child when talking about the show that she was about to put on. "I am so mental and sleepless and excited for this tour," she admitted in an interview with *Billboard*. "This is so different than anything you've seen from me in the past year.

"What's fantastic about [the show] was I was able to plan it while I was on another tour that was on a much smaller scale, opening for the Dolls. This is going to be, like, the ultimate creative orgasm for me 'cuz I'm ready to move on. I'm not restricted to a certain structure for my show anymore. No limitations, I'm free. I want to have a clear schedule of the dimensions for each venue so that we can properly execute all the technology and visuals. I need to mentally prepare days in advance if things are going to be taken out; otherwise, I won't have a good show. . . . Every show's gonna be an A-show by the time I'm done screaming at everyone—'Hang it! Hang everything! Find a place to hang it!' That's gonna be my motto."

Various other themes reappeared in the course of the spectacle. It kicked off with a video titled "The Heart," in which Lady Gaga appears as "Candy" Warhol, dressing up for the show and announcing, "I am Lady Gaga and this is my Haus." Flames begin to spread as the video nears its end, which was the cue for the artist to appear onstage amid her dancers before launching into a performance of "Paparazzi." Video installations come up intermittently throughout in the guise of Candy, while the costumes are everything that might be expected, ranging from futuristic black geometrical dresses to plastic, bauble-decorated numbers and still more along similar lines.

Reviews were slightly mixed, though on the whole positive: "Pop ate the Wiltern in Los Angeles Friday night, thanks to the post-post-post-modernist stylings of dance sensation Lady Gaga, her backpack-wearing backup dancers, and an audience so prepared to match their hostess in sartorial experimentation that it made *Rocky Horror* look like a cotillion. One presumed the Lady approved—and somewhere, to be sure, Andy Warhol stirred in his grave," wrote Whitney Pastorek in *Pop Watch*.

"The tongue-in-cheek tabloid-victim shtick that provides some laughs on *The Fame* grew somewhat tiresome at the Wiltern, especially when the singer started spewing half-baked media-studies nonsense like, 'Some say Lady Gaga is a lie, and they're right: I am a lie, and every day I kill to make it true,'" said *Rolling Stone Magazine*. "Fortunately, this is a woman who knows how to lighten a mood: within ten minutes or so, she'd donned a flesh-colored leotard and a bedazzled admiral's cap and was rhyming 'boys in cars' with 'buy us drinks in bars.'"

The *Hollywood Reporter* liked her: "Before queen of all media Perez Hilton took the stage and proclaimed her 'the new princess of pop,' Lady Gaga showed she's a serious contender to Madonna's crown Friday at the Wiltern," it wrote. "She might be a relative newcomer, but the artist born Stefani Joanne

Germanotta commanded the stage with a royal air during her hour-long set, at times even sporting a glowing scepter."

"The work is paying off," observed the *Chicago Tribune*. "Just weeks into her first nationwide headlining tour, the twenty-two-year-old New Yorker already commands the stage like a seasoned pro."

On one thing most people agreed, however: whatever else you might think about her, Lady Gaga certainly could sing. There was no lip-synching in this particular performance, just as there was to be no lip-synching in any Lady Gaga show, ever. Everything was live on stage: this was the artist in the raw, doing what she did best. And the public just loved it. The opening of Lady Gaga's tour had been a stunning success.

CHAPTER 7

a Storm in a Tea cup

VER SINCE LADY GAGA FIRST CAUGHT THE public's eye, she had meditated, frequently and intelligently, on the nature of fame. And so when, to the great delight of all her friends back in Britain, she returned in April 2009, she carried out something that might well have been an experiment in quite how nonsensical fame can become. Whether or not she did this deliberately is open to conjecture, but for someone as media-savvy as her, it's hard not to suspect that she wouldn't have had some idea of the frenzy she was about to unleash.

It all began on April 17, 2009, when she appeared on the BBC1 show, *Friday Night with Jonathan Ross*. Dressed in a one-shoulder number that appeared to be made from red Post-it notes, Lady Gaga sat backstage as a medley of her hits was played by the show's regulars, 4 Poofs and a Piano, before being pictured taking a sip of tea from a pretty purple teacup. The teacup accompanied her out onstage to meet Ross, who greeted her with a kiss on the hand, commented on the tea and asked about her dress (Lady Gaga confirmed that it was indeed Post-its, before admitting it was actually designer—a couture piece by Singapore-British designer Ashley Isham). She then complimented Ross on his tie, mentioning that its lavender shade matched her teacup.

Some minutes of banter followed, in which she never really appeared to relax. The origins of her name were discussed, along with her burlesque background—when Ross questioned her as to why she would let her father go and see her perform in an Indian headdress and a bikini as she go-go danced to Iron Maiden before setting aerosol cans on fire, she responded primly, "Because it's art"—and added that both parents were now very proud of her.

The chat moved on to clothes and rumors about her on the Internet, including the claim that she was a "well-endowed young man" (this might possibly have been the origin of another publicity stunt that Lady Gaga was to pull later in the year). "If you're well-endowed, I don't know where you're hiding it!" chortled Ross, before Lady Gaga stunned both the presenter and his audience by commenting, "I have a really big donkey dick!"—applause followed.

There then followed an analysis of the phrase "bluffin' with my muffin" in which Lady Gaga calmly informed the audience that it referred to the fantasies she had about women when in bed with an ex-boyfriend: "Oh, good Lord," exclaimed Ross, who was unaccustomed to being upstaged, "I bet he liked it when you told him!" "I never told him," countered Lady Gaga, "but I bet he's watching now." "Blimey!" said Ross.

There was a polite question about the tea she was drinking—"ginger"—before the chat moved on to stage effects, as directed by one Lady Gaga. She spoke about the management's concerns over the problem of getting fog onstage, "Until I told them in New York I used to carry a fog machine in my purse and fog myself." There was another stunned pause from Ross. "No one's ever said that to me before, 'I've fogged myself,'" he said eventually. "I can't tell you how long I've waited to hear those words."

"It's true," said Lady Gaga, who appeared a little taken aback by it all.

Ross then went on to do an impersonation of Donatella Versace, before Lady Gaga scooped up her teacup and went off to change for her later perform-ance, saying of her outfit, "It's metal."

"Of course it is!" replied Ross.

Lady Gaga duly performed, but what gripped the nation's attention—as she must have known it would—was that teacup. Who took a teacup onto a chat show? The world was getting used to some pretty eccentric behavior from her, but even so, this seemed a little unusual.

But that was nowhere near the end of it. Despite the fact that on her previous visit to Britain, the most notable aspect of the teacup was its total absence, by now Lady Gaga seemed to have become so attached to her teacup that she couldn't bear to be without it for one moment. Everywhere she went, she carried that teacup: when she went out to dinner, it was there. Indeed, she then had a teacup tantrum: when she went out to dinner, *avec* said cup, to the Metropolitan Hotel, she accidentally left the cup in the restaurant and had to send out a taxi from her own hotel—Blakes—to get it back again, apparently paying £35 ($55) for the fare in the process.

All of this was, needless to say, avidly reported on. "She kicked up a fuss and demanded someone get her cup and saucer back," said a witness to the teacup tantrum. "She wouldn't drink out of anything else. It just looked like any other cup and saucer to me and said 'Made in China' on the bottom—it seemed a lot of fuss over nothing."

Clearly, it meant something to her (or at least, she was doing a very good job of pretending that it did), however. Bombarded with questions, she came across all coy: "Lady Gaga does not want to reveal anything about the teacup itself, but drinking ginger tea is very good for singers," commented a spokesperson. Indeed it was, but rarely had ginger tea been drunk with such massive publicity attached to it.

Lady Gaga then became jealous of her teacup. "My teacup is so famous," she said. "I yelled at her today, I said, 'You're stealing my thunder, go to bed!'"

But why, implored the public, was Lady Gaga so attached to her teacup? It was, after all, just a cup.

At this, the artist relented. "I used to have tea at home with my mother every day, you see," she explained. "She hasn't got a name [she was talking about the cup again, not her mother], but she's quite famous now so I made her stay in today. I take her everywhere because she makes me feel at home."

And she went on to elaborate further. Not only did it remind her of home, but it was environmentally advantageous, too. "I've made a habit of drinking out of china because it makes me feel grounded," she continued. "I don't think it's a good lifestyle to always be eating and drinking out of paper; it's very wasteful. You know now it's a gimmick and it's just my teacup.'"

A month or so later, she was unfaithful to said teacup: this time, she was pictured drinking out of an alternative one, decorated with red flowers instead.

If ever there was a brilliant example of the nature of modern celebrity, this was it. Lady Gaga mused on the subject of fame in her first album and as she was always explaining to everyone, her whole life was her art. What better way to demonstrate how well she made that work than by leading the nation to become obsessed with a teacup? The fact that it filled the pages of newspapers for days was slightly beyond Warhol: while he had once forecast that in the future, everyone would be famous for fifteen minutes, even he didn't foresee that even teacups could be celebrated for the same amount of time. Lady Gaga could have taken anything—an old teddy bear, an attractive piece of cutlery or a book about self-empowerment—and by the simple fact that she carried it around with her, that item would make the papers.

As for the fact that the object she chose was a teacup, how brilliantly subversive was that? Teacups, in the UK at least, suggest tradition and reassurance; they are symbolic of the British teatime, redolent of their promise that, whatever else happens, the British can always stop for a nice, hot cup of tea. In general, they are not avant-garde items of paraphernalia to be used as props by one of the most media-savvy entertainers to have emerged in the last quarter-century. If Lady Gaga wanted to illustrate the fact that she was quite brilliant at what she did, she really couldn't have carried it off better, had she tried.

The momentous nature of what had happened to her was now sinking in, too. It had all happened so fast and been such a blur that it took her a while to realize quite how famous she had become, but it was when she was performing in Canada that the reality finally hit home.

"I played a show in Halifax a while ago and it was when 'Just Dance' had just hit on the radio big and there were like, 15,000 screaming fans that knew every word, and that's when I knew, I was like, 'Here we go, Canada!'" she related to one interviewer. "I love my Canadian fans. My other big moment was playing San Francisco Pride. It was right after gay marriage was legalized and before all this nonsense started going on, and I was the headliner closing the whole Pride weekend. I remember I got out on stage and the audience was screaming and crying; it was just this really amazing moment.

"Actually, the whole show was running behind so the city shut me off during 'Just Dance' because it's like $10,000 a minute if they don't shut you off. They shut me off during the last minute of 'Just Dance,' my mic went out, the music went off and all my gay boyfriends just sang it back to me. It was the sweetest, most amazing moment."

Although she never said as much, being up onstage and provoking that type of reaction is one way of showing that you are truly loved. In the past, there had been real hurt in her romantic life, however brave a face she might have put on it, but who needed just one person when the whole world seemed to be in love with you? It's possible she could not see that aspect of what was happening to her now—and indeed, given the danger of stalkers, there was a downside to fame—but she was getting all the affirmation anyone could have wanted from the huge number of fans that was rapidly growing.

Meanwhile, the Lady herself was insistent that art was all and nothing else mattered. Despite her astonishing success, she continued to protest that she was not accumulating material wealth: "I plough all my money back into my shows and props," she said. "You could say I'm the Carrie Bradshaw of pop. I am completely poor, but I have a closet full of couture." But her persistence was now bringing in its own dividends: apart from the fact that her outfits ensured she made the newspapers, the spectacular shows were sell-outs and had the punters begging for more.

Whether or not she realized that she was doing it, Lady Gaga was investing for the future all right, and in the best way possible, too. Like all the most successful entertainers, she was turning into a brand as much as anything else, and should she choose to exploit that on a more commercial basis at any time in the future, a further fortune could be hers.

Other artists could only stand back and watch in awe. "Gaga is a bit nuts, but that's the appeal," observed TV personality Alesha Dixon. "We don't know a lot about her, so it would be cool to see if she does anything stripped-back. It's brilliant to storm the charts like she has; it's every artist's dream." That, at least, was an honest assessment. Meanwhile, the cynics were beginning to look more jealous than ever, for Lady Gaga was simply proving herself so far ahead of the pack that she was pretty much in another game altogether.

Her latest obsession became hats: sometimes jaunty little straw numbers that would not have looked out of place at an English tea party (although the rest of the ensemble, usually consisting of some combination of rubber, bra and hot pants, might not have fitted in so neatly) and sometimes objects that were so extraordinarily beyond eccentric that it was hard to know who might have come up with them.

Meanwhile, she appeared on a talk show in the States hosted by Ellen DeGeneres: there was no teacup in sight, but instead a hat that resembled nothing so much as a gyroscope. "It's an orbit. . . . It's my barrier, my Gaga barrier," the Lady explained. She certainly knew how to turn on the charm, though: "It means more to me to be on this show than anywhere," she told the openly gay Ellen. "I look up to you so much. You're just such an inspiration for women and for the gay community."

"And I thought I liked you before," replied Ellen. "Now I like you more." Lady Gaga certainly seemed more at home there than she had on *Jonathan Ross*, but then for all that she and Britain had fallen in love, this is where she really came from. And the all-American success story continued to go down well. "I've been playing piano since I was four and writing music since I was thirteen," she went on. "I just never gave up, I had lots of rejection—but I had a really great mother."

Around this time, the issue of her sexuality was becoming a thorny one. Lady Gaga had been open about bisexuality, had expressed herself to be deliriously happy when drag queens started doing cover versions of her songs and had, in general, been far more open than most in her situation, but now it was becoming an issue for her. People had been so astounded by her talking openly about sexuality that they rarely seemed to want to hear about anything else, but Lady Gaga was beginning to tire of it. "It's actually something I don't really like to talk about anymore," she told one interviewer. "I'm kind of disappointed by it all. I don't like to be seen as somebody who is using the gay community to look edgy. I'm a free sexual woman and I like what I like; I don't want people to write that about me because I feel like it looks like I'm saying it because I'm trying to be edgy or underground."

How, she was asked, did this attitude compare to Katy Perry's, who was most famous for singing "I Kissed A Girl" back in the days before she hooked up with comedian and presenter Russell Brand? "I mean, look, I know Katy and she's super nice, and I don't want to say anything bad about her music or her," replied Gaga (as if she ever trashed other artists). "I'll just say not in terms of Katy but just in general, I'm very careful about the way I write about sexuality. I push boundaries in everything I do, I have a lot of girl-on-girl in my short films, there's a lot of boy-on-boy onstage. I do all kinds of stuff like that, I do not want to make anyone feel used. I'm not trying to use my gay fans to get a fan base: I really, genuinely love them and that's why I made the decision very early on to not play 'Boys Boys Boys' in the clubs right away. I didn't want it to be seen like I was trying to promote a song that was like a gay club anthem.

"Not because I don't wanna have a gay club anthem: I want all my songs to be gay club anthems, I want the whole show to be one giant gay club anthem, but I just didn't want to be seen as the girl who is just using her gay songs to get out there. Anybody that writes music that touches on sexuality or gay anything is setting themselves up to be a target for questioning and interrogation, but I appreciate when people ask me those kinds of questions so I can tell it how it is."

Certainly, it was a brave stance to take. And everything she did continued to make news. In April 2009, Lady Gaga's penchant for skimpy clothing nearly landed her in Russian police custody, however, when she turned up in public wearing even less than usual on a brief trip: "They tried to arrest me in Russia," she wrote on her Twitter page. "But all is calm in the Red

Square, as I leave the east Paris-bound." In Paris they loved her, as well they might: apart from speaking a little French, Lady Gaga was the queen of fashion in a country in which couture is as highly revered as art. If ever a person and a place were made for each other, this was it.

Meanwhile, chatrooms continued to resonate with speculation that Lady Gaga was really a man in drag. For a woman who showed off so much of her body—as Jonathan Ross pointed out, there wasn't anywhere to hide anything that shouldn't have been there—it came as a surprise to find people so suspicious, but then her background was New York's underground scene. It was filled with transvestites and transsexuals, many with pretty extreme looks, and so that might have been why the rumors started—although she was soon enough to use them to her own advantage.

In the interim, she remained quite patient about it all: "I am a lady," she stated simply. "I'm not quite as outrageous as I look—underneath all this I am deeply moral and actually a really nice girl. I look so wild, but I'm not. In the bedroom I like to wear pearls around my neck—I really am a lady." In itself, the comment about pearls might have been dangerously subversive, although Gaga was too much of a lady to point out why.

And she certainly was pretty wild when it came to

the men that she admired. She expressed an attraction for the rock star Marilyn Manson: "I think he's amazing," she declared. "I just have this weakness for leather, long hair and a dark side—maybe that's not such a good thing. I have a problem in that I always go for wild boys. I like long hair, leather, I like a bad boy. I go for these guys, but it never ends well!"

It seemed her admiration was reciprocated. "I was most impressed by her paparazzi photos," said Manson. "I thought that it looked the way that rock stars should look, as exciting as something that Warhol or Dali would do. And I don't consider her to be similar to her contemporaries—the other girls that do pop music—simply because she knows exactly what she's doing. She's very smart, she's not selling out; she's a great musician, she's a great singer and she's laughing when she's doing it, the same way that I am."

If truth be told, although she continued to talk of being bound to her art to the exclusion of all else, Lady Gaga had quietly acquired a boyfriend for herself. An LA businessman, he went by the name of Speedy, and the two met on the videoshoot for "LoveGame." Both were keeping very quiet about it, but people were beginning to notice: "She was caught kissing him on the set of her 'Paparazzi' video," said a source present at the time. "And the next day he picked her up for a date at a sushi restaurant. She isn't very keen on showing her feelings, but there is definitely electricity between them."

Perhaps Speedy had become the recipient of a pair of her trademark false eyelashes. "Whenever I have a lover, I leave them in their apartment on the pillow," explained Lady Gaga. "Kind of like a keepsake." But it was still the music that preoccupied her most. "Speedy means a lot to me, but my music's not going to wake up tomorrow morning and tell me it doesn't love me anymore," she said, after admitting they were indeed an item. "So I'm content with my solitude, I'm OK with being alone—I choose to have someone in my life when I can."

And Lady Gaga was not about to change her mind. "I don't have the same priorities as other people," she revealed in another interview. "I just don't. I like doing this all the time, it's my passion. When I'm not doing a show, I'm writing a song or I'm on the phone with Dada, yapping about a hemline. The truth is, the psychotic woman that I truly am comes out when I'm not working. When I'm not working, I go crazy."

She had now become fond of explaining that she was continuing a great line of artists: "My ideas about fame and art are not brand new," she said. "We could watch *Paris Is Burning* [Jennie Livingston's 1990 documentary about New York drag artists], we could read *The Warhol Diaries*, we could go to a party in New York in 1973, and these same things would be being talked about. I guess you could say that I'm a bit of a Warholian copycat. Some people say everything [in music and fashion] has been done before and to an extent, they are right. I think the trick is to honor your vision and reference, and put together things that have never been put together before. I like to be unpredictable, and I think it's very unpredictable to promote pop music as a highbrow medium."

She certainly was unpredictable. Meanwhile, work continued to top the agenda. The usual bizarre assortment of outfits carried on, including, with a nod to Madonna, a see-through catsuit teamed with a crucifix. Then there was the time when she boarded a plane in New York with short blonde hair and arrived in London with long pink hair. And there was the purple, all-in-one sequined catsuit. Lady Gaga was accused of copying Beyoncé . . . Girls Aloud were accused of copying Lady Gaga. . . . Everyone was confused.

On another occasion, for a twenty-hour flight to Sydney, where she was still supporting the Pussycat Dolls on tour, Lady Gaga teamed gold hot pants, a bra and a pair of strappy sandals. On arrival she threw a white jacket over the ensemble, but there was such pandemonium when she appeared at the airport that a man in the crowd of waiting fans was arrested.

At this point in her career she was, however, forced to take the threat of crazies rather more seriously. Celebrity alone is enough to turn some people into stalkers, but when the celebrity in question spends her time flying around the world half-naked, even if it is all for art, then she runs the risk of some really unpleasant characters turning up along the way. And so Lady Gaga had been forced to acquire a bodyguard, an ex-Marine, and her back-up dancers were also enlisted to help when matters got a little out of hand.

Nor was it just the crazies. A parody of "Poker Face" (called "Butterface") appeared: it showed a lithe young woman, with an excellent body and long blonde hair that totally concealed her face, writhing around until the hair was pulled back to reveal the terrible truth:

> Before I turned around
> You were thinking that I'm a ten,
> But my body's like a Barbie,
> and my face is like a Ken.

It was very funny, but very, very cruel. She herself laughed when shown the footage—what else could she do? Still, it must have hurt a little. The song was not denying she had talent—it was mocking her for her looks, something any woman would find hard to take.

Not that she exactly aimed to calm matters down. In New York, clad in a see-through bodysuit, with only a bra and G-string underneath, she went shopping for tortellini in Stop & Shop, causing a near-riot.

"Why don't you have a fucking 'Meet and Greet' in the frozen foods aisle?" asked Speedy.

And she was more in demand than ever. One day she was shooting an ad campaign for MAC, another appearing on ABC's *Dancing with the Stars*, constantly flying all over America and the rest of the world— nothing succeeds like success. She might have appeared more than a little eccentric to many eyes.

And there was another commitment never to lip-synch, complete with Warhol reference. "I'd never even think about it," she declared. "The whole point to me is, if you're going to be number one, you better *really* be number one! If you're going to be on top, you better be able to do all those things, because it's a real privilege to be able to make music everyday, and I get away with a lot. Andy Warhol says art is what you can get away with, and I get away with a lot with my music and my clothes, and I work really hard, so I could truly be a real artist for all my fans. That's really wrong when you lip-synch."

There was also that determination to be Lady Gaga, come what may. She had created this new persona and the artificial had become real. Well, sort of. "I don't ever want to be grounded in reality," she explained. "In my show I announce, 'People say Lady Gaga is a lie, and they are right. I am a lie and every day I kill to make it true.' It's the dream of my vision, it's the lie that I tell, whether it's an umbrella or it's a hat, or it's the way that I shape my lipstick. And then eventually it becomes a reality. My hair bow was a lie and now it's true."

It made sense—in a way.

Her insistence at always being seen styled to the nines made perfect sense in another way, too. As mentioned earlier, she harked back to the glamor days of Hollywood and the stars back then wouldn't have dreamed of allowing their public to see them with a hair out of place—it would have ruined the mystique. And so it was with Lady Gaga: she had created this extraordinary, fashion-obsessed persona, and she certainly wasn't going to spoil it by letting the public see her looking like a slob.

"That's a very dangerous precedent, and it's not fair to my fans," she stated, and she was right. "They don't want to see me that way just like I don't want to see Bowie in a tracksuit—he never let anyone see him that way. The outlet for my work is not just the music and the videos: it's every breathing moment of my life. I'm always saying something about art and music and fame, that's why you don't ever catch me in sweat pants."

Towards the end of May came the moment when Lady Gaga was officially accepted into pop aristocracy, courtesy of appearing on the cover of *Rolling Stone Magazine* clad in a dress that appeared to be largely composed of a Perspex corset and Perspex bubbles. Her hair was a mass of blonde frizz, her lips a painted purple heart. It was all very seventies. She tackled head-on the issue of whether or not she was sexy: "I don't feel I look like the other perfect little pop singers," she remarked with commendable understatement. "I think I'm changing what people think is sexy."

And there was a lot of truth in that. For a start, despite the cruelty of the parody "Butterface," she had plenty of adoring male fans who thought she was the sexiest creature ever to walk this earth. And she presented herself in such radically different ways, too: one day she looked like an alien, the next she was Marilyn Monroe. She was extraordinarily adept at using her face and body as a canvas, able to project hugely differing images, depending on the mood. Then there was the fact that she was extremely intelligent, not always a prerequisite in a babe, but she was clever and didn't attempt to hide it. That was pretty new, too.

What's more, she was honest, committed and passionate about what she did. Maybe she went on about it, but great artists—and in the field of pop music, that is what she was turning into—have a tendency to become somewhat preoccupied with their work, and so it was hardly surprising that she so constantly emphasized what she was about and what she wanted to do. And there was this determination to make it in the longer term: now she'd got to where she was, she was certainly going to hold on.

"Personally, I just want to keep making art and keep being healthy," she said. "It's not my job: it's my life! I enjoy doing this stuff. Sometimes I meet artists who are like, 'Oh my God, I can't wait to go on vacation,' and I'm thinking to myself: my life is on the road. I'm not on the road waiting to go home and live my life; I'm on the road, living my life, having a fucking great time, making art, staying inspired, calling the Haus of Gaga back in the California and telling them, 'Hey, I saw this amazing piece in a museum, and I wanna do this and I took a photo—let's do this!'

"I'm so in it for the work, I just love it. Next year, I just wanna keep upping the ante for myself as creator and keep getting better and better. In the next ten years I want to have a museum installation!"

She probably would, too.

CHAPTER 8

DIVINE
DECADENCE

S THE YEAR MOVED ON, LADY GAGA SIM-
PLY became ever more outrageous. Every
time it seemed she had excelled herself,
either in what she said or what she wore,
she just upped the stakes one further and made the
headlines again. The next to feel the heat of Gaga were
the Jonas Brothers, the toothsome American trio who
wore promise rings, signifying they had pledged to stay
pure until marriage.

"I love the Jonas Brothers, they're very talented,"
Lady Gaga observed. "I met them once, I'd like to have
a foursome with them."

There might well have been good reason for the
posturing. Her next single in the UK was to be
"Paparazzi," which was the third there and the fourth
in the US—originally, it had been planned to release
another song, "LoveGame," but this was considered
too controversial, even for her. Ironically, however,

Lady Gaga was becoming a victim of her own success: such was the nature of the intensive interest in her that although the song and accompanying video were not due to be released in the UK until the summer (and fall in the States), downloads started to appear on the internet as early as February 2009. Gaga, who was plotting her march towards global domination with an attention to detail that would have shamed your average military strategist, was not amused. "Stop leaking my motherfucking videos!" she posted on her Twitter page, but even this was a compliment of sorts—the "video warranted more than a simple leak; it deserved a red carpet," said *Rolling Stone Magazine*.

"Paparazzi" was to be released in early July in the UK, several months hence, and the video for this (directed by Jonas Akerland) featured three young men, one of whom bore a strong resemblance to Gaga herself. They were, in fact, a Swedish band of three brothers called Snake of Eden, the Jonas Brothers presumably unavailable, and Lady Gaga was seen nestled among them, looking very content.

It was the first in a new series of videos for Lady Gaga, which was to reach spectacular apotheosis with "Bad Romance," in which a story was told to the soundtrack of the song. The video, which weighed in at seven minutes, kicks off with the diva in bed with a man, who leads her out onto a balcony, where he starts kissing her. When Lady Gaga realizes the paparazzi are watching, a struggle ensues, ending with the lover pushing her over the edge.

Mercifully, she survives: she is pictured first in a wheelchair and then on crutches, clearing the way for another innovative dance routine. After she completely recovers, wearing a yellow-and-black number that resembles what would happen should Dolce & Gabbana meet Minnie Mouse, she approaches her lover in a tearoom (the purple cup from *Jonathan Ross* is present) and pours poison into his juice, thus killing him. A call to 911 ensues, in which she is heard saying, "I just killed my boyfriend." Shots of newspapers proclaiming her innocence abound: she is escorted through the paparazzi masses, while the saga comes to an end with a raunchy pose for a mugshot.

Jonas Akerland was a canny choice: he was also the brains behind Christina Aguilera's "Beautiful" and "Smack My Bitch Up" by The Prodigy. In Lady Gaga's case, it was once again a meditation on the subject of fame, in this case what lengths a person might go to in order to become famous. As ever, she pulled the whole thing off with tremendous panache. "Paparazzi" proved to be the most critically acclaimed of all the tracks from the first album while the video was deemed innovative, memorable and fun.

Rolling Stone Magazine loved it. "After a sumptuously shot make-out scene complete with Swedish dialogue, Gaga is thrown off a ledge by her boyfriend as the paparazzi lens click away during an homage to Alfred Hitchcock's *Vertigo*. And only then does Gaga launch into her newest *The Fame* hit," they wrote.

She herself felt as passionately about it as everything else that she created. "It has a real, genuine, powerful message about fame-whoring and death, and the demise of the celebrity and what that does to young people," she said. "The video explores ideas about the sort of hyperbolic situations that people will go to in order to be famous: most specifically, pornography and murder. These are some of the major themes in the video."

As for the song itself, when told there were various different ways of looking at it, she was delighted. "Well, I'm so glad there are a few different interpretations, that was the idea," she continued. "The song is about a few different things—it's about my struggles, do I want fame or do I want love? It's also about wooing the paparazzi to fall in love with me. It's about the media-whoring, if you will; watching ersatzes make fools of themselves to their station. It's a love song for the cameras, but it's also a love song about fame or love—can you have both, or can you only have one?"

The critics loved it. "The fame-obsessed ballad 'Paparazzi' showed how adept she could be with her range," said Jill Menze of *Billboard*. "You may quickly tire of hearing the album's theme constantly reiterated, but the tune of 'Paparazzi' takes up residence in your brain and refuses to budge," wrote Alexis Petridis in the *Guardian* (he was becoming quite a fan). "[It] salt and peppers with a nasty, club-friendly feeling of fun and feistiness that an excellent, well-produced dance album should have," observed Ben Norman on About.com.

The song was released in the United States in September 2009, reaching number six, which placed Lady Gaga in the company of Christina Aguilera, Beyoncé and Fergie as the only women of the century so far to have four singles from their debut album get into the Billboard Top Ten. In the UK, it reached number four.

In the meantime, plans for the show were advancing. There was so much demand for tickets that venues had to be upgraded to hold much larger audiences: "Oh, you have no idea!" Lady Gaga chortled to one journalist. "The tour we're about to announce is such a dream that I have to pinch myself every day to remind myself that it's happening. When you travel the world five times, it changes you. I write all my own music, so as I'm travelling and I'm on this whirlwind of an experience, I'm becoming a better songwriter."

She was, however, having some time for a private life, managing to fit in a quick holiday in Hawaii (ironically, she hit the beach covered up in a T-shirt). But the stories continued to swirl. The next came courtesy of

The Noisettes, whose album *Wild Young Hearts* and single "Don't Upset The Rhythm (Go Baby Go)" were released at the same time as *The Fame* and "Poker Face," and duly suffered as a result: they were pretty generous about it all.

Scotland's much-loved T in the Park festival was coming up and Noisettes' frontwoman singer Shingai Shoniwa had a pretty eye-catching idea of her own: "We will have to set up a big, mud wet T-shirt fight between me and Gaga," she said. "People keep asking if we are touring together because it was spread around the internet. To entertain us, while doing interviews we say we're supporting her on tour but we were chart rivals for the record and single and she beat us both times, so maybe we'd have to play different ends of the stadium and see who wins."

Meanwhile, the Lady herself was in Seoul, clad in harlequin-style leotards and heels, launching *The Fear* in South Korea. There was no let-up to her schedule: she was criss-crossing the world over and over with the kind of schedule that might have punished a far more established performer, much less one who had only been in the mainstream for about a year. "I'm taking every minute I have to myself to write music and be in the studio," she revealed excitedly. "I don't have much time to relax, but I don't have much time for celebrities either, so I'm happy. The only thing I am concerned with is being an artist. I had to suppress it for years in school because I was made fun of, but now I'm completely insulated in my box of insanity and I can do what I like."

"Box of insanity" was one way of putting it. Her next appearance—about two days later—was in Toronto, this time sporting a purple leotard. Next came a bra that fired pyrotechnics (this was to become something of a staple over the next few months). After that was Glastonbury, although that year it was somehow overshadowed by the news of Michael Jackson's death. Lady Gaga was so moved by the tragedy that she cancelled all her press interviews.

Indeed, she was so upset that she refused to leave her tour bus all day. There was actually a personal connection: Jackson had recently been doing some work with RedOne, which brought it home all the more. "Gaga was hysterical with grief," said a source, who was there. "She could not be consoled and spent the day on the phone to her producer RedOne in America. They penned hits 'Poker Face' and 'Just Dance' together. He had been working with Michael on new material recently and was beside himself."

Indeed, the whole festival was highly shaken by the news. Many of those attending made their way to the Stone Circle, at the heart of the area, where they held a candlelit vigil for the dead star. "Jacko Lives" was spray-painted onto the sides of tents and carved into the mud, of which there was a lot as it had been raining immediately beforehand.

Glastonbury founder Michael Eavis acknowledged the somber mood and compared it to the Worthy
Farm Festival of 1970, just after Jimi Hendrix died:
"People hammered signs in the ground all over the
place: 'Hendrix Lives,'" he recalled. "I think people are
aware of the value of superstars. When they die, like
Elvis Presley and Hendrix, everyone misses them. A
superstar is gone and can never be replaced."

But this was Glastonbury, the festival to end all
festivals, and the crowd couldn't stay down for long.
Nor could Lady Gaga. She was in her element, sched-
uled to play on the Other Stage, and anticipation was
building up for the act. And when she did take to the
stage for an hour-long set, she was beyond doubt one
of the high points.

"I used to go to festivals, get naked and take
acid!" she shrieked to the enraptured crowd, before fitting in five changes of dress, including a transparent
bubble number and the pyrotechnic bra, and singing as
she hung upside down. She also wore her exploding
bra. With this kind of showmanship it was hardly surprising the audience adored her, roaring approval as
her set came to an end.

Indeed, she was everywhere. Not only was she the
talk of Glastonbury, but revellers could actually be
heard singing "Poker Face." And when they weren't
singing it, Lady Gaga was—via practically every bar

and café on site. Nor did she fail to show her appreciation: introducing "Just Dance" to the crowd, she told them, "I'll never forget getting the call, telling me I was number one in the UK." This got more cheers, with many singing along at stages during the set.

There continued to be a few people with reservations, however. Among them was Radio 1 presenter Nick Grimshaw. "I'm quite intrigued to see her live," he said. "When she was on at Glastonbury, I went to see Jack Peñate and a friend went to see her. They said it was a mix of goodness and awfulness, and she set her bra on fire. When I interviewed her, she wasn't rude but she really takes herself seriously. She thinks through questions and doesn't take herself for a laugh; I prefer someone more easy-going. Maybe it was her first time in the UK and she was trying to make an impression."

More likely, she really did take herself seriously, and by then so too did the music crowd. There were still some people who were expecting her to make a mess of the set, despite the fact that she'd been touring the world and entertaining internationally for months now; instead they got the highlight of the festival. "Where to start?" asked the *Guardian*. "Lady G wore five costumes, including Union Jack-branded bondage/biker gear, a see-through bubble coat, a glass dress that made her look like Paul Stanley's mirror guitar and others too fruity to describe in detail here."

At the other end of the media spectrum, the *Sun*

was equally enthusiastic. "Wacky pop diva Lady Gaga wowed the crowd with a stage show like something you'd see in a glitzy arena rather than a dirty festival," it observed. "Gaga appeared from a silver case to start the show with 'Paparazzi' and played all her hit songs. But the biggest cheer came when the crowd got a good look at her buttocks as she stood, playing a guitar-shaped keyboard on a revolving stage. Ms Gaga definitely didn't strike a bum note with the audience."

Gigwise even coined a new phrase, "breast pyrotechnics," to describe the event: "Lady Gaga brought her breast pyrotechnics to Somerset as she performed on the opening day of the Glastonbury festival," it announced. "The American singer stunned audiences at Worthy Farm with an array of costume changes during her set on The Other Stage."

One particularly revealing number included a mini-dress that appeared to be covered in mirrored disco balls: it was so high at the back that it afforded a fairly comprehensive picture of Gaga's bottom. Another had her in a red number covered in spikes: for this she was accompanied on stage by two mopeds. Yet another was a black outfit, her nipples all but revealed. During the show, she played a "keytar" (a piano held like a guitar)—this was classy entertainment, however you looked at it.

There is no way that the events of the past year would not have wrought some change in her personality, though. Although she hit the ground running, even she couldn't have imagined the impact that she would have, and to be greeted with a combination of hysteria, number one singles, constant front-page exposure and all the other attention must have changed something about her. She believed it had given her a new level of self-confidence, although she had never exactly come across as the retiring type.

"Because that's your fame," she explained. "That's where your fame lives . . . my luminosity, my constant flashing light. It's in my ability to know what I make is great. I know it is: I know it's great, and it's that sureness—that sureness is infectious." All this was a way of saying that she was good at what she did, but then she was, and the audience's reaction was testament to that.

In the wake of Glastonbury, there was a rare blunder, however. Lady Gaga was due to perform in Manchester as a supporting act to Take That, but pulled out of the performance shortly before she was due to go on stage, claiming exhaustion. The fans weren't happy and nor was Take That's Gary Barlow: "Gary Go got us out of a real spot," he said of her replacement. "You should have heard me backstage."

But in fairness, given the amount of careering around the world that she was doing, Lady Gaga could be forgiven for having an off day. She was clearly so thrilled at having fulfilled her dream that she wanted to pack in every minute she could, but she was only human. Besides, she returned to the stage after a couple of days: "Make me a star, Man-ches-star!" she cried. Barlow relented: "The tour is going brilliantly and we will have Lady Gaga back supporting at the weekend," he remarked. "It's a shame she was poorly and couldn't play Manchester"—although, of course, she subsequently did.

Her audience responded in kind. "A fan got this amazing tattoo, a massive Lady Gaga tattoo that was very intricate and detailed," breathed Gaga. "In it, I was wearing this crystal outfit, but this thing was like an art piece. I was so flattered because tattoos are for life. I should imagine that most pop stars don't experience that kind of gesture. I was a really big tattoo all the way down his arm. Pretty rock'n'roll."

Writing in the *Guardian*, Dave Simpson assessed her appeal and that of the shows perfectly. "Flitting between a racy black bra to a dress apparently made of glass, Gaga is a pop cyborg, a robot Debbie Harry/Edie Sedgwick creation with a voice the size of China," he wrote. "She has two default modes. Like the early Material Girl, she sells aspiration—songs address being 'beautiful, dirty and rich' and claim, 'it's good to live expensive,' a factual statement from a girl who went to the same school as Paris Hilton.

"And she sells sex. When she compares Manchester to 'a good fuck' and waggles a seemingly naked bottom, you fear for the souls of the younger children in the crowd. Like Madonna, she reveals everything but actually tells us nothing."

That much was true. For a performer who frequently exposed a good deal of flesh, and for a highly intelligent woman who was able to analyze her own art and the very concept of the fame that she had conjured up, who really knew what lay at the heart of Stefani Germanotta's soul? The fact that she had created a stage persona using a totally different name did not mean that Stefani herself was no longer there: for a start, for someone who talked so much about sex in general terms, she could be remarkably coy when it came to specifics. As for what motivated her, she had never really properly explained this. She wanted to be Andy Warhol, or a twenty-first century version of him, yes; she was eager to make art and to elevate pop music to the level of high culture—but why? And then there was the fact that in among the other personae, she was actually a Catholic convent schoolgirl. Anyone who thought that her exhibitionist tendencies revealed all there was to know was missing the fact that there was a lot of mystery surrounding large chunks of her life.

And so the circus continued. First came an appearance in support of Gay Pride at London's G.A.Y. nightclub—four costume changes, including a pink latex rubber number and a lipstick scrawl on her stomach—and then it was on to Malta for an MTV special.

For this, she sported a mask. "It's an art piece," she explained. "The Grim Reaper inspired my look." After that came a fashion shoot for *Maxim Magazine*, with the usual revealing outfits: some PVC teamed with black lingerie. If she was trying to maintain public interest in her, she was going about it in the right way.

Meanwhile, the explanation of her life philosophy went on, centered around her next album, *The Fame Monster*, which was to be released in the autumn. The Grim Reaper seemed to be the current fad. "I have an obsession with death and sex," she said. "Those two things are also the nexus of horror films, which I've been obsessing over lately. I've been watching horror movies and 1950's science fiction movies. My re-release is called *The Fame Monster*, so I've just been sort of bulimically eating and regurgitating monster movies and all things scary.

"I've just been noticing a resurgence of this idea of monster, of fantasy, but in a very real way. If you notice in those films, there's always a juxtaposition of sex with death, that's what makes it so scary. Body and mind are primed for orgasm and instead, somebody gets killed; that's the sort of sick, twisted psychological circumstance."

Next stop was Cork, where she played The Marquee, clad in her silver disco-balled dress; the crowd went wild, especially when she changed into her pyrotechnic bra. She was by now touring with

Kanye West as an equal, as he himself explained: "She's talented and so incredible that she's not an opening act. We're doing it together, with no opening act," he said, displaying a level of generosity not always found in the performing community. Indeed, Lady Gaga returned the compliment: "I'm married to Kanye, I love and admire him so much," she said. "As I say, we're married."

Natalie Horler of Cascada wasn't quite so enthusiastic. The group released a new single in the summer of 2009, "Evacuate The Dancefloor," which was widely compared to "Just Dance." This was clearly meant as a compliment, but she herself didn't agree: "I can't really stand people comparing the song to Lady Gaga," she said. "I love her music, but think it's silly as we've been around with this sound for so much longer, whereas Gaga is a new artist. I can't hear the similarities myself."

But that wasn't the point: Lady Gaga was the hottest thing around. To be compared was nothing to be sniffed at, even if you had been on the scene a lot longer.

Various demands, sensible or otherwise, continued to be reported in the press. Lady Gaga was playing the music festival in Punchestown, in County Kildare. It was rumoured that she'd requested a pink helicopter to get her there, on top of which she had now booked a seat on the plane for her outfit alone.

"Lady Gaga has an absolutely amazing outfit designed for Sunday's show," revealed a source. "But she was worried it would get damaged on the plane and refused to allow it to be sent over in the hold luggage. It cost her over 3,000 euros to get made up—the hat alone was 1,000 euros. So she has told organizers to book her an extra seat on the plane and she will lay out the costume on that. It's going to cost a fortune, but she's insisting on doing things her way because she takes her image so seriously. Everyone was very surprised when the request came through, but it seems nothing's too crazy in the world of Lady Gaga."

It wasn't that crazy. Quite apart from the fact that it made sense to look after her stage costumes, that sort of thing created mystique. Lady Gaga was one of the most famous couture fans in the world: how better to illustrate this than by buying your dress a seat on the plane? And this kind of story kept her in the news: chances are, she couldn't have cared less whether her helicopter was pink, grey or black—but she understood the value of image. There was nothing crazy about that.

Nor was there anything crazy about her fashion sense. Not only did it keep her in the news almost the whole time, as well as being another crucial component for her mystique, but at some point in the future, with the launch of a clothing line, it looked set to be commercially advantageous in more ways than one.

"I dress like this all the time," she explained yet again. 'For me, it's self-expression. When I'm going to meetings about secret stage show things, I might be in some baggier latex, but for the most part, vanity is just a self-choice. It's not a negative thing. Everybody is vain, even if you don't have a ton of make-up on and you're just wearing a sweatshirt, that's the sweatshirt you choose. There's a reason that you like that one. We're planning to eventually mass produce and sell everything. But for now, it's more like me adding things into the show, piece by piece, and incorporating the disco ball into fashion, as opposed to just the actual prop."

And she continued to plough the money she'd earned back into the shows, saying: "That is like, infinitely more important to me than a Mercedes. In Italian, love is *te voglio bene*—which means, I want good things for you. I think that with fame comes a lot of people that are jealous, and with success comes people that want things from you. The key to having both is surrounding yourself with people that want good things from you. For love? I don't know—I've never really had it. I think it will be somebody that does not dim my shine, but that makes it brighter. And when mine is bright, lights up his or hers, or whoever."

She was on the verge of sounding wistful, not a mood often associated with her. But T in the Park in

Paisley, Scotland, was coming up shortly and so she could take her mind off things by preparing for yet another show. There were a few other, very famous female performers at the festival, including Katy Perry and Lily Allen, but as usual, Lady Gaga effortlessly stole the limelight from the moment she arrived onstage clad in a silver leotard and announced, "I am Lady Gaga and this is my home."

With that, she launched into "Paparazzi," followed by "Beautiful, Dirty, Rich" and then "Just Dance," for which she donned a denim-studded leotard. That was not the last of the leotards: a jewelled one followed for "Brown Eyes" before she ended with "Poker Face." The audience went ballistic as she curtseyed and was, quite literally, carried off the stage.

Katy Perry wore almost as little as Gaga, so much so that the two of them became sources of fascination for Johnny Borrell of Razorlight. "Johnny looked like he was on a mission," said a source. "He was glued, watching the girls perform."

Almost immediately afterwards, Lady Gaga appeared at Oxegen on July 12, 2009, where there was a panic when she discovered she hadn't brought the right underwear to dance in and was forced to ask the organizers for help. "We had to get an artist liaison officer to scramble out to Naas today and frantically search the clothes shops for the underwear," revealed an Oxegen source. "It definitely goes down as the strangest request we have ever had from an artist at the festival. Gaga said she needed the underwear for her and her dancers because of the kind of dance moves they do on stage. She had forgotten to pack it herself and only had a couple of hours before her set. But she put on a great show and perhaps the pants saved the day."

The buttocks were on display again, prompting a wry comment from Florence Welch of Florence And The Machine. "Usually I put on weird outfits," she said. "I have been known to run around in sparkly pants, but I cover my actual buttocks, unlike Lady Gaga. But she is sexy and has a great bum."

She certainly was up to her usual tricks, shouting at the crowd, "Scream until you make me have an orgasm!" It wasn't for the fainthearted, but they lapped it up.

Besides, she was going from strength to strength. There were suggestions she might be asked to act as a judge on *The X Factor*: "I've never been asked to be a judge, but I wouldn't say yes, if I was," said Lady Gaga rather primly (and anyway, she was proud not to have emerged from reality TV shows). "I don't believe it's right to judge music—it's so personal. Right now I'm possessed with this incredible instinctual energy to write joyous melodies. I don't know where it's coming from."

The ability to attract headlines seemed to be no problem for her, too. Back in London, where she told diners at Balans in Soho that she "gets so lonely in Britain," she was spotted wearing a straw boater, rose-tinted spectacles and white lacy gloves. The teacup was nowhere to be seen, but a Pudsey bear was in evidence. Next, she was pictured partying with TV producer David Hasselhoff and then played the Brixton Academy.

She might have been lonely, but she was certainly loved and commentators were beginning to think she might just last the course yet. Preparations were now underway to launch *The Fame Monster*, a re-release of the earlier album with some added tracks, and it would produce probably her best (and most popular) hit to date.

But Lady Gaga barely got through a day without some controversy or other coming to light, and now a very odd one indeed was emerging. Some very strange pictures had surfaced from Glastonbury, showing Gaga with an appendage lacking in the vast majority of female pop stars. Was it possible the strange rumors were correct and that Lady Gaga wasn't a woman at all, but a man?

CHAPTER 9

IS SHE, OR
ISNT HE

THE SUMMER OF FESTIVALS WAS COMING along nicely. As usual, Lady Gaga was keeping everyone entranced: she updated her fans by twittering, and the latest was this: "In every minute of the day, the truth is that I'm dead, until I'm here onstage with you, then I'm alive instead."

Well, at least it rhymed. She was still roaming around Europe and now turned up in Ibiza, where she played at Eden and Wonderland (where she jumped out of a Dalek). Then it was on to Vienna's Stadtpark and from there to Hamburg and Copenhagen: the touring was non-stop. Even she appeared to be feeling the strain: with a complete absence of Speedy on the horizon, she revealed, "If anyone had told me at the start of my career what success brings along with it, I would have thought twice. Now I know you have to choose between fame and love; both together won't work.

Sometimes, I feel my fans are all I have."

But there was no chance of her giving it up now. It had been announced that Lady Gaga had nine nominations in the upcoming MTV Video Music Awards (as had Beyoncé, a fact much commented on in the press). Finally, Gaga admitted that the teacup episode really had been thought out in advance. "I wanted to say something on a real level about fame," she explained. "I decided to take a purple teacup out of my china collection and take it to London and make it famous. I put it in videos and had fans pose with it, and put it on TV." She'd certainly made her point—through a few weeks of constant exposure, she'd made that teacup the most famous teacup in the world.

Despite the fact that she'd just admitted to quite deliberately stoking up massive publicity about something completely trivial, the world still fell for the next one which, as far as publicity stunts went, was beyond anything that she had managed to pull off yet. A video had emerged of her recent concert at Glastonbury, in which she was seen to be getting off a motorbike. She was wearing a shirt so short, even by her own high standards, that it didn't quite cover something which few female pop stars could claim to have. The footage was grainy and the object in question not easy to identify, but given its place on her person, it appeared quite unmistakably to be a male appendage. And so the question shot across the internet: was Lady Gaga, in fact, a hermaphrodite?

As seasoned Gaga watchers would know, there was a background to all this. First, there had been rumors that she was a man well before the picture surfaced, probably because she had emerged from the New York burlesque scene, hung out with transsexuals and transvestites, and had the kind of dress sense frequently associated with drag queens, but that just meant she was an original performer. Then there was the fact that Jonathan Ross and various others had brought the subject up, possibly setting off an idea in Lady Gaga's head about testing the waters to see what would happen if she really did appear to have a penis.

But before everyone got too carried away, there was a third point as well: Lady Gaga was the most media-savvy woman on the planet. If anyone knew how to generate publicity, it was her, and if she really had a penis that she didn't want to reveal to the world, there was no way she would have allowed herself to be photographed in such a revealing dress. This wasn't a woman like Princess Diana who, nearly thirty years earlier, was caught unawares when she was pictured in a skirt rendered see-through by the sun: this was a woman who spent every waking moment working out how next to shock and awe.

Added to that, she'd been cavorting about half-naked for a year now, wearing such tight-fitting and revealing garments that it simply would not have been possible to keep the penis out of sight, had it existed. It didn't—it *couldn't*. Initially at least, no one wanted to believe that, however.

As chatrooms buzzed with speculation about what might or might not be hiding under Lady Gaga's skirt, there was a further development. A quote surfaced, purporting to be from the Lady herself: the origins have never been traced. No one knew for sure whether she'd really said it or not (and knowing Gaga, it was entirely possible she had arranged for the quote to be discovered online), but it was certainly taken seriously in some circles.

"It's not something that I'm ashamed of, just isn't something that I go around telling everyone," Lady Gaga is purported, although it has never been proven, to have said. "Yes, I have both male and female genitalia, but I consider myself a female. It's just a little bit of a penis and really doesn't interfere much with my life. The reason I haven't talked about it is that it's not a big deal to me.

"Like, come on! It's not like we all go around talking about our vags! I think this is a great opportunity to make other, multiple-gendered people feel more comfortable with their bodies. I'm sexy, I'm hot: I have both a poon and a peener, big fucking deal!"

Whoever actually said this, it didn't really matter: it simply increased the intense and growing interest. Lady Gaga herself did not, initially, comment—she didn't need to. Staggeringly huge amounts of publicity were building up without her having to do a thing about it, but what was even more shocking was that, post-teacup, no one could see that, whether or not the stunt was deliberately planned, they'd been had.

It was in early September 2009, in Australia, that Lady Gaga finally chose to comment on the furor in a radio interview. Perhaps she realized that if she didn't do something to stop the wilder rumors, then this would dog her for the rest of her life—as indeed, it still might. But being Gaga, she didn't do anything so straightforward as to deny it: "My beautiful vagina is very offended," she announced primly. "I'm not offended: my vagina is offended! I'm not embarrassed—I sold four million records in six months; I'm not embarrassed about anything. I think this is society's reaction to a strong woman. The idea that we equate strength with men and a penis is a symbol of male strength, you know; it is what it is. But like I said, I am not offended at all, but my vagina might be a little bit upset."

Was that what it was really all about: to make a statement about the purported power of the penis? Forget that Lady Gaga is a performance artist at your peril—it should always be remembered that her current performance was her whole life. Perhaps she just wanted to test the waters to see how people would behave towards her if they really thought she had a penis. Then again, maybe she was just having a laugh. And then again, it might not have been planned at all. Perhaps she'd picked something up, or dropped it or been photographed at some awkward angle; there were any number of other possibilities. But was she a hermaphrodite? No.

One of the reasons behind her reticence might have been pure mischief: Lady Gaga was perfectly happy to watch the world at large make fools of themselves by claiming she was a hermaphrodite against the physical evidence that just about everyone had caught a glimpse of, and indeed, sheer common sense. But another reason, of course, was the background from whence she came. Gaga couldn't possibly claim it was an insult to be thought a hermaphrodite or transsexual for the simple reason that she mixed with so many others who were and therefore she ran the risk of insulting them. Besides, by now she had other fish to fry.

Above all else, though, the story created a huge amount of publicity and there really was no star alive better able to appreciate the importance of this. As has been noted earlier, one of Lady Gaga's earliest fans was the massively influential blogger Perez Hilton (who, incidentally, also created an artificial persona of his own with a nod to Paris Hilton) and it was all the publicity that he generated for her, putting her up on his site over and over again, that helped turn her into an international star. Gaga knew she owed him, too.

"Perez Hilton is brilliant to me," she admitted.

"Because he's taken something that people don't think is valid, don't think is important, and he's made them obsessed with it. People are obsessed with him: they're obsessed with his site, they're obsessed with what he does. They love him, they all love him: they love you, they hate you, what you don't want is indifference. The day that I put a record out that nobody says a damn thing about, that's bad!"

But she certainly wasn't in danger of provoking an indifferent response with her next project. Lady Gaga had just recorded a new video, "LoveGame," in which she is seen cavorting with both sexes, including a woman dressed as a policeman. (She also wears a leotard that reveals so much that the hermaphrodite rumors seem sillier still.) Her relationship with her own sexuality appeared to be getting more complicated by the day: although she was happy to talk about the desire for the occasional girl-on-girl action, she was not a lesbian at all, really (or so it seemed). The world she came from was not so much that of gay women but gay men.

"The real motivation is to just turn the world gay," she explained to one interviewer. "I very much want to inject gay culture into the mainstream. I committed myself to them and they committed themselves to me, and because of the gay community I'm where I am today. I feel intrinsically inclined toward a more gay lifestyle: I myself am not a gay woman, I am a free-spirited woman. I have had boyfriends, and I have hooked up with women, but it's never been like 'I discovered gayness when I was dot, dot, dot.'"

So that was clear, then. But she was being perfectly serious about it all. She was about to embark on a tour of the US with Kanye West and warned him that her popularity in the gay world could have a knock-on effect for him: "I just want to be clear before we decide to do this together: I'm gay," she said. "My music is gay, my show is gay, and I love that it's gay. And I love my gay fans and they're all going to be coming to our show, and it's going to remain gay." West didn't appear unduly concerned.

Another of Lady Gaga's theories was that her success was in part due to the tumultuous time that America and the West had just been through. "Somehow I feel, socially, after a war or after something really bad happens, there's a rebirth of naiveté," she remarked. "That's when the fame monster is born. My whole life is a performance: I have to up the ante every day." That was certainly true enough, and she was succeeding, too.

Indeed, "LoveGame" upped the ante in Lady Gaga's videos. In many ways it was not one of her best; the works that have really stood out are the ones that tell a story, like "Paparazzi" or "Bad Romance." But "LoveGame" succeeded in paying tribute both to the New York club scene, through the music and the lyrics complete with the disco stick reference, and indeed to Michael Jackson, given that, like his video for "Bad," it was set in the New York subway. Gaga's third single in the States and her fourth in the UK was released around the world, too, where it was banned from prime-time viewing in Australia due to the sexual nature of its content.

"LoveGame" was directed by Joseph Kahn; as usual, Lady Gaga gave it her all, in the making and the explanation afterwards. "This is all part of a movement," she explained. "My artistry is much deeper than fashion or anything like that. I love pop music and I want to bring it back. People are truly hungry for this: they generally miss the nineties and the superfans flooding Times Square, crying and wailing, and doing anything to see the fingernail of a star. I want that back and the 'LoveGame' video is just another move towards that.

"'LoveGame' is a genuine New York lifestyle video—it's got that feeling of 'gay, black New York,' of inclusion and glamor. I wanted to really bring forth the girl that I was four years ago and I wanted to put it in the setting of the underground subway. I worked with Joseph Kahn and he did an amazing job: he didn't just capture the fashion, he captured the artist."

It was certainly one of her more controversial offerings, although she was quick to defend the work. "LoveGame" might have been a little obvious, she admitted, but it wasn't half as raunchy as some of the other material that was coming out. "I don't think disco stick is subtle," she said. "It's very clear what that lyric is all about. If anything, I happen to think people are frivolously hard on me. A lot of youth-oriented pop music is much racier than mine. 'Throw me on the floor, take off my clothes, give it to me, baby, let's dirty dance.' All these records are so provocative, but it's the context of what I'm doing that makes people concerned. It's the music in relation to the visual, in relation to the way I move and the way I articulate the lyrics. But if I wanted to make music to make people sing 'la di da' that would be very boring."

But Lady Gaga couldn't do boring: it simply wasn't in her nature. And the reception to the track was fairly positive. It had "a gutter level quippage with sinuous moves," said Sarah Rodman of the *Boston Globe*. "It has all the winning ingredients of its predecessors: a radio-friendly, club/electropop feel; a provocative, yet silly enough catchphrase and hook (Let's have some fun, this beat is sick/I wanna take a ride on your disco stick); and a dash of eighties synth magic, so the adults can play along. On 'LoveGame' Gaga is in it to win it," said *Billboard* music editor Chris Williams.

"The robotic 'LoveGame' with its brilliant line 'I want to take a ride on your disco stick' is brilliant, but utterly cold and leaves us awarding Gaga the yearbook title of 'pop star most likely to kill,'" said

Talia Kraines rather perceptively on BBC online. Meanwhile, Daniel Brockman, music editor of *The Phoenix*, felt that the increasingly famous line was "the trashiest yet awesomest refrain I've heard on a major record label this year." And to conclude: it was "top-notch, diamond encrusted pop," said Ben Hogwood from MusicOHM.com.

Despite its controversial content, the "LoveGame" video was generally considered a great success and the Lady herself was definitely pleased. "I wanted to have that big giant dance video moment; I wanted it to be plastic, beautiful, gorgeous, sweaty, tar on the floor, bad-ass boys, but when you got close, the look in everybody's eyes was fucking honest and scary," she told *Entertainment Weekly*. "The whole idea behind the subway 'Bad' [Michael Jackson's song] thing is that me and my friends from New York, we're all, like, the dopiest fucking artists: best designers, performance artists, dancers.

"The dancers in the video, those are not hot LA people that you see in everybody's video. Those are kids who don't get cast, because they're too fucking real. I love the imagery of a downtown, bad-ass kid walking down the street with his buddies, grabbing a pair of pliers and making a pair of sunglasses out of a fence on the street. I thought that imagery was so real and it shows that no matter who you are, or where you come from, or how much money you have in your pocket, you're nothing without your ideas. Your ideas are all you have. The opening of the video is me with this chain-link hood and these intense glasses; they look so hard—it looks like I plied them right out of the fence and put them on my face." What did everyone else think? Well, they tended to concentrate on the fact that she was seen kissing another woman.

Professionally, life couldn't have been better. She did a photo shoot for the gay magazine *Out* that had her climbing out of a grave with strips of leather around her waist: she was posing as "a kind of Frankenstein's bride who gets attacked by a sexy vampire and then becomes one herself," revealed the shoot's photographer, Ellen von Unwerth.

Privately, matters were not so happy, though. Lady Gaga was learning that while male success causes no problems as far as relationships are concerned, the same cannot be said when a woman achieves fame and fortune. She had now split from Speedy, and although some people liked to portray her as a heartless man-eater, in reality she was hurt.

"Do you know the feeling of your heart being so terribly broken you can feel the blood dripping out?" she asked rather dramatically. "When you have felt this, only then will you know how I'm doing."

No one was entirely sure what had gone wrong. Some felt that Speedy was upset when he'd seen a picture of Lady Gaga kissing another man, but then she

Lady Gaga collects the Best New Artist Award at the MTV Video
Music Awards on 13 September, 2009. She was nominated for nine
awards in total, including Video of the Year, Best Female Video and
Best Pop Video.

Showing off her softer side, Lady Gaga joined the Orange RockCorps volunteers at Body Positive (an HIV support centre) and painted a mural of herself.

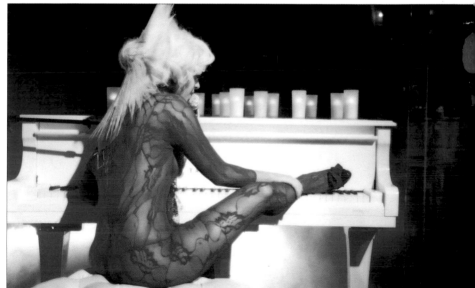

Not just Queen of Pop but also Queen of Fashion, Lady Gaga performs at the after party of the Marc Jacobs Spring-Summer 2010 show in a suitably wacky outfit and hairstyle.

Fashion icon: Lady Gaga works the trends for peacock feathers, leather gloves and sheer material all in one outfit at the Billboard Women in Music Brunch.

Fashion icon: Rocking the gothic look with exaggerated shoulders and big sunglasses, at the launch of her Heartbeats headphones at HMV Oxford Street.

Above: Lady Gaga performs at the Human Rights Campaign National Dinner in Washington, DC.

Below: On Saturday Night Live, the 'Ryan Reynolds' episode.

During the episode of Saturday Night Live, Gaga also got to perform alongside the original Queen of Pop – Madonna.

With such eccentric fashion taste, Lady Gaga rarely pleases everyone. But her bold, daring style makes her unique – and we wouldn't want it any other way.

Above: A photo compilation called 'Worst Fashion of the Decade' sees Lady Gaga join Bjork and Christina Aguilera.

Below: Another – this time showcasing the new trend of underwear-as-outwear – puts Lady Gaga with Melanie B of the Spice Girls and Christina Milian.

seemed to spend almost her whole time kissing other men—it was part of her life's work. There was also the long-distance nature of the relationship, of course, never easy to deal with, plus the fact that Gaga was becoming so incredibly famous. Often it is hard for a man to form a relationship with a woman of a higher status and Lady Gaga was well on her way to achieving the same kind of acclaim as Madonna and Michael Jackson. Fame and success have their downsides.

There were rumors that her ex, Matthew Williams (aka Dada) had staged a comeback: they were certainly seen getting up close and personal on a flight. But a source close to Gaga just laughed it off. "There's nothing going on between her and Matthew, but they are still very lovey-dovey—that's just how she is with everyone," she explained. "But they're definitely not back together. She is very much single and on the lookout! It's been really hard for her recently as she's been on the road constantly and hasn't had friends around her, so she has been feeling lonely. She just enjoyed the comfort from Matthew, who's also her creative director."

And she certainly hadn't lost the desire to shock. When she emerged from a plane at Heathrow in August 2009, it was with fangs and fake nails attached in order to give the photographers a brand new look. But then, as she explained in an interview, in many ways she'd always been like that: it's just that now she had the fame and the wherewithal to indulge herself. In many ways, her entire life had been leading up to this point.

"For a little while, I thought girls were just jealous, which is why they were mean to me," she said of her childhood. "Maybe they were jealous of my fearlessness, but I think I genuinely used to rub people in the wrong way: I'd talk about things and do things that were very ostentatious and over the top, and very vain. And it's part of my artistic aesthetic: I think you're born an artist, it's like being gay—you're born gay, and then you discover that's who you are over a period of time in a world where maybe being gay is not the normal thing. Then you look it in the eye and you say thank you, and you put it in your heart and you lock it up and you go.

"When you're twelve years old and making clothes with plastic flowers attached to them, and trying to choreograph shows at your school that are entirely too sexy—you start to be like, 'OK, this is my aesthetic.' My aesthetic is in so many ways exactly the same as it was when I was younger, I'm just smarter. And I know how to execute the ideas—and I have a bigger budget."

She was spending that budget in increasingly interesting ways, too. Late August saw a photospread for *FHM* magazine, in which she was pictured in a black leather bodice, while it was rumored that she now wanted to acquire a bulletproof piano, whatever that might be. This was followed by a shoot for *V* magazine, taken by the acclaimed photographer Mario Testino: in some shots, clothes were dispensed with altogether, Gaga's modesty protected only by a few pieces of pink fluff.

"Mario wanted me naked all day long," she revealed. "It was my stylist who kept sneaking in the designer stuff—we love clothes. But Mario understands me and he said, 'I want this to be about you, I don't want it to be about the clothes.'"

The photo shoot was newsworthy not just because of the photos in which Lady Gaga looked as if she'd taken to bathing in fake tan, but because of the photographer behind the lens. Mario Testino is one of the aristocrats of the photography world, famously shooting Princess Diana at the height of her glamor and fame, and to be photographed by him was an honor indeed. It was a mark of how far she'd come in such a short space of time that she was now posing for Testino— who made her look stunning in the process. There was, incidentally, no sign of a penis, either.

The pictures were glamorous and sexy, very much in keeping with the image Lady Gaga was cultivating for herself, although she was well aware this could be a double-edged sword. After months in which debate centered on whether she was a hermaphrodite, a lesbian, both, neither, or, as seemed the case, relatively mainstream in her physicality and her desires, Gaga knew all about the power of sex, but it could pose as many problems as it could help boost her image.

"Being a woman in the pop world, sexuality is half-poison and half-liberation," she said. "What's the line? I don't have a line. I am the most sexually free woman on the planet and I am genuinely empowered from a very honest place by my sexuality. What's more primal than sex? I mean, it's so honest. If I didn't think I had the talent to back that up, I wouldn't have done it."

And she had a point. "LoveGame" might have been one of the most sexually explicit songs and videos ever to appear in the mainstream music charts but it was critically acclaimed and a work of real talent, even if it wasn't to everyone's taste. Lady Gaga might have been trading on her outrageousness, but she was certainly able to back it up.

In early September, she made musical history when it was announced that she was the bestselling artist ever in the five-year history of the singles download chart, with "Poker Face" and "Just Dance" selling almost 1.5 million copies between them. She was back in the UK to launch her "Heartbeats by Lady Gaga" headphone line and if she was still ruing the fact that success made a happy love life difficult, she was not showing it—"My life is a marathon and I'm not ready to take a sip of water yet," is how she put it to one journalist.

There was a great deal of teasing in the press when, out and about in New York and Berlin, Gaga was pictured in clothes that actually covered her crotch—by no means always a given—but she herself was totally unrepentant about her style. It was more a statement than anything else and she could be brutally honest about how she sometimes appeared, even to herself.

"I just don't feel that it's all that sexy," she said. "It's weird—and uncomfortable. I look at photos of myself and I look like such a tranny, it's amazing! I look like Grace Jones, androgynous, robo, future fashion queen. It's not what is sexy. It's graphic, and it's art, but that's what's funny. Well, yeah, I take my pants off, but does it matter if your pants are off, if you've got eight-inch shoulder pads on, and a hood, and black lipstick and glasses with rocks on them? I don't know. That's sexy to me. But I don't really think anybody's dick is hard, looking at that. I think they're just confused and maybe a little scared. It's more Manson to me than it is sexy."

One of the biggest differences between Gaga and some of the others on the music scene was how seriously she took it all. Of course, most stars naturally view their own careers in a pretty serious light, but for Lady Gaga, the intrinsic worth of what she was doing was just as important to her as anything else. She constantly talked about art and again, all the naysayers who pointed out that while her pop songs were very good, they were still just pop songs and no more than that, were missing the point: her life was her art.

Oscar Wilde once famously claimed that while he poured his talent into his work, he reserved his genius for his life and Lady Gaga was turning out to do much the same. Her whole existence—pace the teacup episode—was becoming an extended observation on the society in which we live and our obsession with celebrity and fame. Gaga was doing far, far more than wearing a few wacky outfits and penning a couple of good tunes: she really was turning the mirror back into the faces of everyone who so eagerly watched her every move.

"If somebody said to me, 'What you do isn't art,' I would say, 'They're right.' Yes, it is, no it isn't; absolutely, perhaps, it's irrelevant, it's important. That's what this is all about, really," she commented. "For me, more than anything, I want to do something important. It's gotta be important. If it's coming out of my mouth, if it's going on my body, if it's going on TV, it better be important!"

Strangely, in some ways she actually played down what made her so unique. Quite correctly, she observed that she wasn't exactly the first singer to take her clothes off in a music video, but it must be said she brought a very individual touch to it all. Sometimes, though, it seemed as if even she had tired of having to cope with all the criticism so frequently aimed in her direction, particularly about the amount of flesh so often on display.

"Just because I have underwear on in a video— you could say that's 'Justify My Love,' that's Britney in her 'Womanizer' video, you could say it's Grace Jones," she observed. "Women have been taking their clothes off in videos since the eighties. Lita Ford, Dale Bozzio, Blondie. . . . I mean, not to be so direct but I just think that people need to come up with better references than Christina and Gwen and Madonna all the time. There's so many other artists that have been provocative for decades."

True enough, but they simply weren't up to her standards. Nor were many of the women she mentioned exercising control in the way that she was. And while Lady Gaga might have cited Blondie as another cultural reference, Debbie Harry and Co. did not have the long-lasting career that Gaga was hoping to attain for herself. "I'm not trying to prove to anybody that I'm going to be here for thirty years," she said. "You either are, or you're not. You either have passion for it, or you don't. It's either important for you to stop, and buy a condo and have babies, and marry a rich actor, or not do any of that and continue to make music and art, and die alone—which is what I'll probably do."

There it was again—that slight note of yearning

for a life that she didn't have, namely one that included a partner. She could have dealt with it all, of course, by giving up the career and returning to New York to be an Italian-American mom, if that was what she really desired, but it wasn't really what she wanted at all. Lady Gaga was eager to be bigger, brasher and more successful than anyone else, ever.

Whatever she did, she would continue to provoke controversy, upsetting a good many people in the process, but she also managed to cultivate even more admirers for herself along the way. And her next shocking appearance was right now.

CHAPTER 10

THE DEMISE OF
LADY GAGA

NE OF THE GREAT PROBLEMS WITH MAKING a name for yourself as the most shocking and provocative woman out there is that you must constantly keep outdoing yourself. A single extraordinary appearance is not enough: you have to top it with something bigger, better and even more unexpected. Lady Gaga had managed to do all this through her appearance but now the stakes were getting higher and something more was required.

In September 2009, one of the highlights of the music industry calendar, the MTV Video Music Awards, came around. Even before the ceremony itself, the Gaga publicity machine spun into action: there were reports that while Beyoncé and other stars contented themselves with requests for scented candles and chicken, Lady Gaga had requested the presence of a lion to accompany her on the night! Who knew if there was any truth in the story? It wouldn't have been out of character, although in the event no lion showed up.

In the course of the evening, she was to manage less than five changes of outfit, each one more revealing than the last. The first, which she paraded for the red carpet, was very demure by her standards, although she stood out from a mile away. She was dressed in a long, black silk creation from Jean Paul Gaultier, with a dragon-print underlay and lacy covering. This was teamed with a striking Keko Hainswheeler neck brace and, slightly more controversially, a gold eye patch, making her somewhat resemble the Phantom of the Opera, plus a black lace trilby. She was also seen exchanging a kiss with Kermit the frog.

Once inside, Gaga got on with doing what she did best. She stripped off to a white two-piece ensemble complete with thigh-high white leather boots and started to perform "Paparazzi," which is when she completed her masterstroke: pretending to stab herself in the chest. Fake blood streamed out everywhere as Lady Gaga rubbed it into her face, before collapsing into the arms of her backing dancers. Moments later, she reappeared, hanging from a cord with her neck twisted to one side.

It was a masterly performance. In a room full of exhibitionists, the biggest exhibitionist of them all had done it again: the stunt was extensively reported in the press, alongside a good deal of tut-tutting from anti-suicide campaign groups, who felt that she really had gone too far this time. But that wasn't an end to it. Her next outfit was all red: red lace, including a red lace face mask which she took off when she collected the award for Best New Artist. She then sported a white bikini with a circular snowflake mask, before a final change into a silver leotard. In all, it was quite a night.

The evening's host, Russell Brand, certainly thought so. "Lust is one of the deadly sins, so there was no lust," he said. "Did you see Lady Gaga when she had on the bird's nest and was wrapped up in that head-to-toe lace outfit?

"She's incredible. I'd be all over that, she's amazing! Imagine what it must be like—I'd like it if she came home, acting up like that. You'd never know where you are; your mood would change from one day to the next. I bet she'd go all night, swinging from a chandelier."

Robbie Williams was another admirer. "I think Lady Gaga is a great pop star," he declared. "She's an ace pop star—she could be the new Madonna, if she doesn't slag it up too much. Madonna did slag it up, but not as much as Lady Gaga—she's very entertaining."

Inevitably, there was some sniffing about her choice of outfits as well as the controversial performance, but who cared? Gaga had done it again. She had the whole world talking about her, one of the planet's most famous lotharios was lusting after her and on top of that, she'd been named Best New Artist. "Paparazzi" achieved two awards, as well: Best Art Direction and Best Special Effects. What wasn't there to like about that night?

The clout that she now wielded in the music industry, and the wider world, was becoming increasingly evident and anyone who hadn't got the message could hardly avoid it when she teamed up with the President of the United States. Lady Gaga had taken up the cause of gay rights and so in October 2009, she performed at the Human Rights Campaign National Dinner, which was held in Washington just before the National Equality March.

"It's a privilege to be here tonight to open for Lady Gaga," President Barack Obama wryly observed. "I've made it."

The Lady herself was in unusually somber style. Eschewing her usual underdressed look, she wore a long black dress and dark glasses to sing John Lennon's "Imagine," with the lyrics slightly changed to refer to the murder of Matthew Shepard in 1998. After they beat and tortured him, college student Shepard was killed by a pair of homophobes. His death has since become a focal point for the Gay Rights Movement: his parents, Judy and Dennis Shepard, were awarded the Edward M. Kennedy National Leadership Award at the dinner. As for the song she chose—"In the music industry, there's still a tremendous amount of accommodation of homophobia, so I'm taking a stand. I'm not going to play one of my songs tonight, because tonight is not about me," Lady Gaga told the audience. "It's about you." The second verse was also changed:

> People of the nation:
> Are you listening?
> It isn't equal if it's sometimes.
> I want a real democracy.
> Imagine all the people
> Could love equally. . . .

There followed a speech at the National Equality March: "Are you listening?" she asked President Obama. "We will continue to push your administration to bring your promise to reality. I will never turn my back on my friends. Today is not a one-off performance."

This all went down pretty well with the gay community. The *Washington Post* published an article entitled, "FOR GAY ACTIVISTS, THE LADY IS A CHAMP," in which it was reported that the gays present at the dinner practically overwhelmed her, giving her two standing ovations, and she also received the credit for the fact that the 3,000-strong dinner sold out so quickly.

"Primarily, the kids that are taking to the streets are eighteen, nineteen, twenty, twenty-one, and she is their Madonna, their Cher, the next-generation diva, so to speak," observed Ross von Metzke, editor of Advocate.com. "She puts her time and money where her mouth is."

All this partly came from her background, of course. Lady Gaga had spent her formative years as a performer in an atmosphere full of gay people and so she had witnessed firsthand how difficult so many of them had it in life. Gay men had also been her first audiences, supporting her when she was just another stage-school kid with dreams, turning up to see her, urging her on. And now it was payback time, something she was only too enthusiastic to embrace, taking up the cause of gay rights with fervor, and so they loved her all the more.

It wasn't long, though, before it was back to business as usual. "I don't really go in for wearing underwear," she told one interviewer. "Not very much, no: it's rare that I decide to put some on. There's no point really, and I'm not ashamed of it."

Meanwhile, the plaudits continued to flood in. *Billboard* held its annual Women In Music Brunch in early October, which she attended, wearing a see-through dress decorated with feathers and human hair:

"Twelve months ago, I would never have imagined being here and receiving this award," she remarked—for yes, Lady Gaga was given the Rising Star of the Year award.

"She's provocative, fearless and most importantly, a prodigious songwriter," said Bill Werde, editor in chief of *Billboard* magazine, as he introduced her.

"I didn't expect to be accepted into the pop community like I have been," admitted Gaga, sounding genuinely choked up. "With help from radio program directors, the gay community, fans and people like *Billboard*, we had a remarkable year. Thank you from the bottom of my heart."

She was about to launch her next single, "Bad Romance," of which more shortly. In the run-up to the event she went through another ritual in the initiation into show business aristocracy: a tussle with Madonna. Unlike Britney Spears and Christina Aguilera, both of whom got to smooch the Queen of Pop, the pretender to the title was to engage in a catfight. It took place on *Saturday Night Live* when Kenan Thompson (aka DJ Dynasty Handbag) introduced "Two exciting entertainers, performing together for the very first time." The two walked on, with Lady Gaga wearing black bra and knickers, Madonna in a black corset and both sporting over-the-knee black boots: "What's wrong, Madonna, can't get into the groove?" taunted Gaga.

"What the hell is a disco stick?" retorted the diva and the two women started pulling each other's hair, before being separated by the DJ.

"Hey, guess what, Madonna? I'm totally hotter than you," Gaga continued.

"What kind of name is Lady Gaga? It sounds like baby food!" snapped Madonna in return.

At this point, Thompson intervened to encourage them to kiss and make up. As both puckered up, he leaned forward and received the kiss himself.

OK, so it wasn't a display of Wildean wit, but it amused the audience and gave Lady Gaga yet more exposure: various costume changes heralded the chance to play more of her hits, including the next one, "Bad Romance."

"Bad Romance" was to be the first single from *The Fame Monster*, the re-released first album with eight additional tracks. Those tracks were further meditations on fame, although in this case, the downside of it. Gaga had been famous for long enough to see that it had its problems, as well as its delights: the very term "monster" was testament to that.

"On my re-release, *The Fame Monster*, I wrote about everything I didn't write on *The Fame*," she explained: While travelling the world for two years, I've encountered several monsters, each represented by a different song on the new record. I spent a lot of nights in Eastern Europe and this album is a pop experimentation with industrial/Goth beats, nineties' dance melodies, an obsession with the lyrical genius of eighties' melancholic pop and the runway . . . I wrote every piece on the road—no songs about money, no songs about fame. I wrote it for my fans, so I wrote everything in between."

"Bad Romance" and its accompanying video were probably her best work yet. Her latest song was to turn into a massive international hit, deservedly so, while in many ways it brought together everything that made her what she was now. An incredibly catchy number, it showed her intellectual side in a number of references to Alfred Hitchcock: it involved high fashion, the plot of the video was reassuringly crazy and the costumes even more so—everything came together quite perfectly.

Such was the interest in all that she did now that a demo version had already leaked onto the internet, prompting Lady Gaga to twitter: "Leaked next single is makin' my ears bleed. Wait till you hear the real version." And it was worth waiting for. Brief snatches were played on programs such as *Saturday Night Live*, but the real premiere was at Alexander McQueen's spring/summer show at Paris Fashion Week in October—fittingly, as Gaga wears a McQueen outfit in the video.

The cover art came out shortly afterwards, with a very striking image of Lady Gaga's blonde hair peeking above the maroon transparent gauze that covers her face. Even that was a hit with the critics: "It must be said that Lady Gaga is maintaining her hitting streak of generating powerful images to accompany her music and stage presentations," wrote Bill Lamb on About.com.

The main gist of the song revolves around the idea of writing a "bad romance" story with all the clichés about "needing" and "wanting" someone, but there is far, far more to it than that. For example, there's the Hitchcock reference about wanting someone's "psycho," which Gaga herself explained thus: "What I'm really trying to say is I want the deepest, darkest, sickest parts of you that you are afraid to share with anyone because I love you that much."

On the whole, the critics loved it. "Lady Gaga's singing is at its best so far here as she moves from threatening to floating sweetness, and back again," wrote Bill Lamb. "If you had any fears that Gaga would be a one-album flash in the pan, the room-filling beats and melodies of 'Bad Romance' should help dispel them." "It's particularly hard to resist the Jabberwockian catchiness of the 'Bad Romance' hook," observed Christopher John Farley in *The Wall Street Journal*.

"Synth-powered 'Bad Romance' is a ferocious club thumper with a sordid underbelly," pronounced Edna Gunderson in *USA Today*. It was one of Lady Gaga's best yet, said Michael Hubbard from MusicOHM, "mainly because it seems to contain at least three separate sections, each as catchy as the last." It had "wicked sex appeal," according to Monica Herrera of *Billboard*.

"If melodies could be time-stamped, this would have eighties branded on its ass," declared Sal Cinquemani from *Slant* magazine. And so it went on.

CHAPTER 11

a GLIMPSE
OF GENIUS

"**B**AD ROMANCE" SOARED ITS WAY UP THE chants as the quite exceptional video went out. It was directed by Francis Lawrence, who had worked with numerous international stars, including Britney Spears, Janet Jackson, Jennifer Lopez and Gwen Stefani, while the Haus of Gaga managed the art direction. Michael Jackson always said that one of the secrets of his s   u   c   c   e   s   s was that he worked with the very best, and now that was what Lady Gaga was doing: "I knew [his] ability as a director is so much higher than what I could [do]," she said.

Indeed, she couldn't have made a better choice. "I wanted somebody with a tremendous understanding of how to make a pop video, because my biggest challenge working with directors is that I am the director and I write the treatments, and I get the fashion and I decide what it's about, and it's very hard to find directors that will relinquish any sort of input from the artist," she continued. "But Francis and I worked together: it was collaborative. He's a really pop video director and a filmmaker. He did *I Am Legend*, and I'm a huge Will Smith fan so I knew he could execute the video in a way that I could give him all my weirdest, most psychotic ideas, but it would come across too and be relevant to the public."

The video kicks off with Lady Gaga sitting, bedecked in gold couture and a pair of sunglasses made from razor blades that she designed herself. "I wanted to design a pair for some of the toughest chicks and some of my girlfriends—they used to keep razor blades in the side of their mouths," she explained. "That tough female spirit is something that I want to project. It's meant to be, 'This is my shield, this is my weapon, this is my inner sense of fame, this is my monster.'"

Her fingernails are covered in wire mesh; she places one finger on the button of an iPod, presses it and the music starts to play.

The video is set in a bathhouse. As the music begins, sunlight floods the room, with the camera panning across a sign that reads, "Bath Haus of Gaga," and a series of white pods start to open, with a central one from which Lady Gaga emerges, marked "Monster." The creatures coming out of the other pods are clad in white latex—their costumes inspired by Max Wolf in the classic children's tale, *Where The Wild Things Are*—which also obscures their eyes, leaving only their mouths free to sing.

The first lines of the song, about wanting "ugly" and "disease," set the tone for what is to follow, namely a group of supermodels drugging Lady Gaga and selling her to the Russian mafia as a sex slave before she exacts a terrible revenge. The latex-clad monsters dance, interspersed with shots of Gaga sitting in her bathtub, where she washes away her sins (Madonna was not the only one to use Catholic imagery in her videos). Suddenly a group of supermodels descend: they pull her out of the bath and force vodka down her throat, before beginning to tear her clothes off. Now dressed in a very seductive diamond-covered outfit, she begins to dance for the group of men watching and bidding, crawling on all fours towards them and straddling one, who promptly ups his bid for her.

Interspersed are shots of Lady Gaga clad in Alexander McQueen, complete with twelve-inch "Alien" heels, striding purposefully across a room as the chorus urges her to work the fashion. She is also seen almost in suspended animation, clad in black two-piece, water seemingly frozen in the air around her, held aloft on a silver sphere; a group of men circle, eyeing up the goods. The action then switches to the bedroom, where the Russian who bought her is sitting on a bed. Sporting a cloak made from a polar bear and dark glasses, Gaga walks purposefully towards him, finally sliding the cloak off to stand in white lacy underwear.

The couture-clad diva cocks her finger and suddenly the bed spontaneously combusts. As it goes up in flames, Lady Gaga watches imperiously; this is interspersed with shots of the diva and her backing dancers all dancing vigorously in lacy red lingerie. In the final scene, Gaga lies, smoking a cigarette on the charred bed, with a skeleton lying beside: her pyrotechnic bra erupts and the video winds to a halt.

The whole production was quite extraordinary: the song itself was one of the catchiest numbers of the year and even without the video, it would almost certainly have been a massive hit, but this was simply outstanding. Everything had been thought through to the last detail: the storyline, the costumes, the dancing. The whole thing worked on a number of different levels, too. There was the basic storyline, of course, of the kidnap and sale into sexual bondage (both dark territory and the stuff of male and female fantasy—Lady Gaga was not afraid to explore the dark side), but also, that added element: the relationship with fame.

Was this the price that Gaga had to pay for the fame she so desired? Did she feel as if she'd had to prostitute herself in some way? The themes were all based around sex, decadence and corruption; alcohol and even cigarettes, twenty-first century society's biggest no-no, were present, and so by implication, if not actually spelled out, were drugs. Then there was the change in her persona about halfway through: she starts out as a young innocent in the bathtub and ends up being a sexually experienced murderess. And although the actions in the video are not quite so explicit as they are in "LoveGame," in some ways the implications are even more so. Lady Gaga crawling along the floor to the man who will eventually become her prey is quite a sight: both predator and victim, an extremely sexualized being.

She looked simply stunning throughout. Shown with both barely there and heavily drawn, as well as couture, make-up, she never looked better than she did in this video and the critics thought so, too.

"I don't think Gaga has ever looked prettier than in the close-ups where she's more stripped down," said Tim Satck in *Entertainment Weekly*, who also drew a comparison with the dancing in Michael Jackson's video for "Thriller." "On the flip side, I love those crazy dilated pupils she sports for much of the video. This video is amazing."

And that would appear to be the consensus across the industry. Daniel Kreps in *Rolling Stone Magazine* went still further, comparing it to the work of the late film director Stanley Kubrick: "'Bad Romance' has Gaga providing fans with perhaps her craziest, brightest canvas yet, all the while dressed in some of the most outrageous outfits she's ever worn (and that's saying a lot)," he observed.

Over at MTV, Jocelyn Vena said she thought the video heralded a whole new era for Lady Gaga. "The old Gaga is over, here's the brand-new Gaga: the one who seems to delight in pushing the boundaries and exploring all manner of sexual proclivities," she declared. "[It is] a testament to her brilliance as an artist that Gaga is using [the video] as the jump-off point for the next leg of her career. These days, it seems like pop stars all too rarely put this much thought into their vision and their products."

No one could accuse her of not thinking things through. "This music video really makes us appreciate everything Gaga actually brings to pop music," said Jennifer Cady from E! "She's exciting to watch, plain and simple. We need someone like Gaga to really bring it. To put actual thought and care into her product so that it feels alive."

"Like the song [the video] blasts at your senses until you are just left drowning in the audio and visual power of it all," said Bill Lamb from About.com. "Lady Gaga continues to break down barriers and take us all to new places. In a music industry that too often seems to want to revisit whatever might have been successful in the past without breathing new material and elements into it, Lady Gaga remains a powerful force to observe."

Meanwhile, it brought to mind some of the greatest stars of them all for Christopher John Farley in *The Wall Street Journal*: "The singer-songwriter-pianist-provocateur seems to be one of the few pop stars these days who really understands spectacle, fashion, shock, choreography—all the things Madonna and Michael Jackson were masters of in the 1980s.

"The theme of the video seems to be something about how fame seduces, addicts and perverts those that attain it. It's an ongoing concern of Lady Gaga, and the idea is all the more curious because she seems to have been obsessed with it even before she was *actually famous*."

In the wake of the release, she appeared on *The Jay Leno Show* (complete with a cream teacup), during which her very presence seemed to cause hysteria each time she opened her mouth. Leno provoked screams from the audience when he pointed out that her musical achievement in terms of chart positions was the first time anyone had managed that since The Jackson 5 "It's been a long time," he observed. "Thirty-nine years," agreed Lady Gaga—while she herself practically reduced the audience to more shrieking, simply by saying, "Hey, guys!"

Leno quizzed her on the subject of the upcoming Grammy Awards. Some of those in the music industry felt that Gaga was being treated unfairly: due to technical issues, she was not permitted to be nominated in the Best Newcomer category, the reason being that she had actually been around for some years now as a songwriter and been nominated before. But given the year she'd had, it was a small price to pay. Indeed, she was wise enough not to belabor the point, eliciting more shrieks and whoops from the crowd when she mentioned that the biggest reward from the last year had been her fans.

"I really don't care about that outside validation," she continued. "My fans are my family now, I just care about what they think."

The interview was highly illuminating. Again, she recounted that she'd been a difficult pupil, before saying that her music had been very different in high school—"I was singing about things like love, things I don't care about any more," she said. As a matter of fact, she was loved as never before—but by her fans, rather than an individual man. Lady Gaga was getting global validation, if not her own bad romance.

Much was also made of the fact that she was to perform for the British Queen. "They asked me," she simply explained. And what did one wear to perform for the Queen? "Latex and fishnets," she replied to yet more shrieks, before pointing out, perfectly reasonably, that if they had asked Lady Gaga to perform, then presumably they wanted her as she usually appeared, not a cleaned-up version of herself.

And finally, Leno ventured onto the subject of the

wild speculation that swirled around her. What was the worst rumor that she had heard about herself? he asked, and there were no prizes for guessing what he was referring to. "That I'm from Yonkers," she countered, keeping an admirably straight face. "I love the Bronx, but I'm from Manhattan."

Her appearance on the show was quite restrained by her own high standards, consisting of black trousers, black boots and a black, silver-trimmed top, although admittedly, it did feature the kind of shoulder pads that wouldn't have looked out of place in *Dynasty*. There was no such restraint when she hopped back to Ellen DeGeneres' show, a year after her first appearance. This time around, she wore a nude-appearance latex dress that was teamed with fishnets, white boots and silver glitter make-up around her eyes, giving the appearance that she was wearing a mask.

Gaga showed she knew how to charm her hostess and work the crowd.

"It's been a year since you were on, and look at you—you're huge!" exclaimed the hostess.

"Not as big as *Ellen*!" cried Lady Gaga, prompting another wildly enthusiastic response from the audience.

It was, however, as Ellen pointed out, a phenomenally steep climb. But Lady Gaga didn't, and never has, appeared arrogant in any way: on this occasion she thanked God and emphasized just how lucky she was. Often a performer's early promise is destroyed when they start to believe their own publicity: canny woman that she was, Gaga wasn't about to make the same mistake.

Ellen correctly identified some of the elements that had contributed to Lady Gaga's success. For a start, she actually sang, even when she was live—unlike so many other stars that relied on lip-synching. And then there was the fact that she put on such an enormously entertaining show: "There's no one else like you," said Ellen (correctly). Indeed, the last artist to have indulged in such spectacle was David Bowie.

They then turned to the subject of clothing, and more specifically, the latex dress.

"Is it comfortable?" asked Ellen.

"It's fashionable," Lady Gaga replied, before adding that the designer had also made the clothes for the "Bad Romance" video. A montage of pictures of Gaga in some of her more outré outfits then flashed up: "Are you dreaming, are you taking some kind of a drug, where does the inspiration for your outfits come from?" Ellen continued.

Lady Gaga identified some of the designers she wore, before setting out her own philosophy. "The whole point of what I do, the monster ball, the music, the performance art aspect of it, I want to create a space for my fans where they can feel free, where they can celebrate, because I didn't fit in in high school, because I felt like a freak," she explained. "So I want to create this space for my fans, where they feel like they have a freak in me to hang out with, and they don't feel alone." This got huge applause.

"This is really who I am, and it took a long time to be OK with that," she continued. "I'm sure you all, and maybe you [to Ellen], you feel discriminated against, and you don't fit in and you want to be like everyone else, but not really—on the inside you want to be like Boy George—I did, anyway. So I want my fans to know that it's OK. You don't always feel like a winner, but that doesn't mean you're not a winner."

"I was a rebel like you wouldn't believe," revealed Ellen. "At high school, in Atlanta, Texas, which is a very small town, I wore outfits—I would be the Lady Gaga of Atlanta, Texas." With that, a photo of the teenage Ellen was beamed up in which she wore a dowdy, long gingham frock.

"It looks great, it's very seventies," Lady Gaga politely observed.

"I was ahead of my time," said Ellen. "But I'd put you in it—I think you could carry it off."

The same picture flicked up again, but this time with Gaga's features superimposed. She took it exceedingly well.

A series of questions was posed. What did she watch on TV? *Ellen*—and sci-fi monster movies. The best Christmas present ever? A four-track recorder from her father when she was eleven, which she could hook up to her piano and record on.

"Be good to your parents," Lady Gaga advised.

It was sound advice, and it was also a key to the real Lady Gaga. She adored both parents, spoke about missing them when she was on the road and had also been fretting about her father, who was about to undergo open-heart surgery and for whom she had written a song, "Speechless."

So that was the reality: underneath all the outrageousness, the wild costumes, the provocative statements, the astounding videos and mind-blowing shows, Lady Gaga was what she had always been—a good, convent-educated Catholic girl, who loved her parents.

You can take the girl out of the convent, but you can't take the convent out of the girl. She hadn't really changed that much, after all.

CHAPTER 12

a Tale of
Two Divas

N THE WAKE OF "BAD ROMANCE," LADY Gaga had somehow entered a whole new league. From the word go, there had been no doubt that she was an original, to put it mildly, but the sheer quality of what she had produced, to say nothing of the fact that it was an international bestseller—again—signified that she really was here to stay. There was something different about "Bad Romance:" it had a compulsive quality about it. You wanted to play it again and again; the video made you like the record all the more, while the record made you like the video.

And in addition to that, it was somehow more humane than some of the other work she'd done. All her other videos were accomplished, but there was no sense of human emotion in them—sometimes quite the opposite. Lady Gaga could, when she chose, and that was frequently, have a very self-contained air about her: a coldness, almost. But there was nothing chilly about "Bad Romance:" it managed to combine the qualities of being funny, weird, moving and sexy, an almost unique mix in the history of pop-music scenes.

The reference to the Queen that she made on television was to the upcoming Royal Variety Performance in Britain, but there was plenty going on before then. It was turning into a stunning end to an amazing year. One newly released statistic after another showed just how far she'd come: the most downloaded, one of the most Googled, the most controversial, the most influential. . . . The effect that she'd had on Planet Celebrity was becoming increasingly obvious, too, with many people copying her look or clearly influenced by it. At that point, a lot of celebrities were referencing looks that centered on a small, high-cut leotard and they also opted for corsets, basques and all the other paraphernalia that had once been Madonna's and Lady Gaga was now making her own. But unlike Madonna, Gaga's prime intent in all her weird and wonderful outfits was not to look sexy, but to look different. Madonna had made herself Queen of Sex; Gaga, while undeniably able to turn on the appeal when necessary, seemed intent on making herself the Queen of Eccentricity. But she was in it for the long run and she knew what must be done to keep fresh in the public eye.

The artwork was released for *The Fame Monster*: fittingly for someone so obsessed with fashion, the shots were taken by Hedi Slimane. Slimane was a French fashion designer, but more specifically, one of Gaga's types of fashion designer: with an Italian-Tunisian-Brazilian background, he studied political science at the École du Louvre, before going on to work for Yves Saint Laurent. After being vigorously headhunted by such prestigious houses as Gucci and Prada, he ended up at Christian Dior before branching out on his own. Photography and design became passions, with Slimane designing album covers for artists such as Phoenix and Daft Punk. Another book, *Stage*, was the first-ever published on the new rock scene.

Indeed, like Gaga herself, Slimane was passionately interested in music and fashion, with both of equal importance for him. He was immersed in the British indie rock scene, counting Pete Doherty and Amy Winehouse among his many acquaintances, while he also discovered Isaac Ferry (son of Bryan) as a model, featuring him in one of his catwalk shows when Isaac was just sixteen. Slimane is credited with starting a few English bands, including These New Puritans and Eight Legs, while his garments, with their thin silhouettes, have influenced the look of many a participant on the British fashion scene. If ever there was a person who was the perfect collaborator for Lady Gaga, it was him.

The image he produced as the cover for *The Fame Monster* was pretty much perfect, too: the Lady's hair was short, bobbed and fringed; it cascaded down and resembled thick straw, standing out with a life of its own. She wore a PVC cape with massive shoulder pads, with one arm out of the cape, looking slim and vulnerable. The rest of her was completely hidden. She held the collar of the cape across the bottom of her face, with only the eyes and nose visible, and what an expression she managed to convey.

There was something in her eyes that was aggressive yet vulnerable, questioning and pleading, triumphant but somehow troubled. All the complexities and ambiguities of Lady Gaga were summed up in that shot. Though it could not be said to be a disconcerting image, it certainly wasn't easily quantifiable, either. It was entirely appropriate for a woman who revealed everything, and yet nothing. That image showed Gaga cloaking herself against the outside world and yet giving viewers direct access to her eyes, the very windows of the soul.

Meanwhile, she was invited to one prestigious event after another: the latest being a performance at The Museum of Contemporary Art's 30th Anniversary Gala in Los Angeles, in front of an audience that included Gwen Stefani and husband Gavin Rossdale,

Pierce Brosnan and Eva Mendes. She was becoming an A-lister among A-listers: if you wanted to have the most happening and fashionable people at your party, Lady Gaga simply had to be there.

And even by her own high standards, Gaga totally excelled herself this time. Her piano, designed by Damien Hirst, was painted pink; her outfit created by architect Frank Gehry, Miuccia Prada and film director Baz Luhrmann. Dancers from Russia's Bolshoi Ballet were in attendance; the whole collaboration was by Francesco Vezzoli, an Italian performance artist known for merging the celebrity and art world. Lady Gaga was in her element: everything about that November night summed up what her life was all about.

"For me, art is a lie, and the artists are there to create lies we kill when we make it true,'" she told one journalist present at the event. "Francesco and I were like warriors on stage, trying to make a true moment. Art is life, life is art—the question is what came first?" In Gaga's case, the two were interchangeable. She had made her life into a work of art. How could the two possibly be prized apart?

There was one minor setback in the autumn: Lady Gaga and Kanye West were due to stage a Fame Kills Tour, but West had disgraced himself at the MTV Awards when he interrupted Taylor Swift's acceptance speech for Best Female Video, saying it should have gone to Beyoncé instead. Gaga was publicly very supportive of her friend, but it caused problems: the Fame Kills Tour was cancelled and another tour, The Monster Ball, was announced in its place instead. This was revealed in Lady Gaga's usual style: "A message to all my little monsters: *The Fame Monster* will come out four days before the first live show," she announced. "You have exactly 96 hours to learn all of the lyrics so you can sing along. Dress accordingly."

The concerts promised quite an experience. "The theme of monsters is certainly going to be an influence," she continued. "It's going to be a truly artistic experience that is going to take the form of the greatest post-apocalyptic house party that you've ever been to." Expectations were high and given the year that she'd had, Gaga clearly wanted to put on quite a show.

Lady Gaga was becoming simply too big to perform with many of the artists with whom she'd been hanging out. She would never have said this herself—she was too astute to make enemies and probably, if truth be told, too polite—but her name was now massively bigger than those with whom she could not have dreamed she'd be associating just a year before. Gaga made no secret of the fact that she'd been putting her work before anything, including a social life and a love life, but now her choice really was paying off. This, of course, created painful decisions, like who she should or shouldn't be touring with.

She was certainly in the A-list now. The next big project to be announced was a duet with Beyoncé. The two had spent much of the past year being promoted as rivals, not least when both received nine nominations at the MTV Awards and also when they sported similar-looking leotards: the obvious next move was to team up. This would have the dual advantage of boosting each other's image (not that either really needed it), as well as showing that far from being rivals, they were the best of friends. Beyoncé was long established, while Lady Gaga probably soon would be—what did they have to lose by getting together? In the end, the result wasn't quite what everyone was hoping for, but the rationale behind the link-up was there for all to see.

Gaga was receiving praise from somewhat lofty quarters, too. Madonna had played along with her on *Saturday Night Live* and now she went one step further, pretty much anointing her as the chosen successor: "I see myself in Lady Gaga," Madonna said. "When I saw her, she didn't have a lot of money for her production. She's got holes in her fishnets, and there's mistakes everywhere—it was kind of a mess. But I can see that she has that 'It' factor. It's nice to see that at a raw stage."

But it wasn't so raw any more. The singles market

in the UK had been soaring, mainly due to digital downloading, and Lady Gaga occupied the top two slots in the first ten months of 2009 with "Poker Face" and "Just Dance." The money that poured in was directed towards the increasingly slick production in the videos and shows: what might once have been raw talent yet to be chanelled into a purer form had now become highly sophisticated stuff. But the Lady was adamant that in no way was she influenced by money, as indeed she had already proved.

Indeed, she loathed the stuff. She continued to shock, and she did so now, coming out with one of the most surprising statements yet from any up-and-coming star.

"And the truth is, there's only one thing in the world that I really, really hate," she told her audience when she was onstage at The Monster Ball Tour, a month or so hence. "Does anyone know what that is? Money! But there's only one thing I hate more than money . . . and that's the truth. I don't like the truth: I like a giant dose of bullshit any day!"

The truth was one thing, but actually loathing money? That really was the mark of an unusual rock star. Except, of course, it was yet another manifestation of where she came from. Lady Gaga had not chosen an obvious route into mega pop success in that hers was the New York art club scene. Had she really been motivated by money, there were any number of different ways that she could have tried to launch herself, but incredibly unusually for a pop star, that didn't seem to be the reason why she was doing it. She was perfectly happy with the fame aspect of it, obviously, but she really did have things to say and ways in which she wanted to express them. She was a very unusual artist.

As Halloween drew near, she decided to swim against the tide and keep it casual. Apart from anything else, there were so many people out there who had adopted her look that she stood more chance of standing out if she didn't actually go completely over the top.

"I'm not dressing up for Halloween," she explained. "I have been unable to go out and have a good evening, get sloppy, maybe ending up laying face-down somewhere in a bar, so I am pretty excited about going out and not dressing up because I have heard that a lot of people are going to be dressing up like me. I'm a whisky girl, so I'll be on that."

The rest of the time, though, it was business as usual. Lady Gaga teamed up with New York fashion label Hello Kitty for a photo shoot in which she wore a dress entirely made up of toy kittens. She was again in her element. "Forgive the pun, but she looked like the cat that got the cream," commented an onlooker. "She was writhing round in the studio and didn't want to take the costumes off! I think Lady Gaga gets off on these crazy outfits, but a lot of people would think she looks like something off an *Alice in Wonderland* film."

Of course she did! That was the whole point, and it was also the reason why companies such as Hello Kitty were so eager to work with her: wherever she went, publicity followed. She had an incredibly keen eye for what would make the newspapers and an increasing number of brands were becoming aware of this, too. Hotness breeds hotness, and the more in demand she was, the more in demand she became. Whether or not she got off on her eccentricity was neither here nor there: what really mattered was her ability to spot a trend and play with it. And in return, the trends seemed to spot her.

Not that it was always easy to dress like Lady Gaga. She suffered for her art: "I arrived recently for a show and the stylist had brought this outfit and the damn thing was like, fucking hundred pounds—head-to-toe, leather, studs," she told one journalist. "And I was wearing this famous Vidal Sassoon haircut, where only one eye is showing. So basically, I did this whole show carrying a hundred pounds, looking out of one eye, dancing—and then my tits explode at the end. It's not as easy as it looks!"

But the fans loved it. The next tribute came from controversial TV sitcom animated series *South Park*, which featured a parody of "Poker Face." It, too, had its own background: the music played over a tale about anti-whaling protestors ditching peaceful protests instead of guns.

Lady Gaga, meanwhile, planned a new tattoo. Her father was recovering from surgery, but his daughter wanted to pay tribute: "I'm gonna get a heart tattoo that says 'Dad' in it," she declared. "He got all teary-eyed and said, 'Well, you're running out of real estate, so don't get it too big!'"

CHAPTER 13

THE REWARDS
OF SUCCESS

TRAVEL WAS ONE OF THE BENEFITS OF LADY Gaga's increasingly successful career. One of the oddities of present-day America is that while almost all the inhabitants are of immigrant stock, the vast majority never leave its shores. Lady Gaga was of Italian heritage and yet until she became successful and started to travel the world, almost her entire life experience was in the United States. That, too, was changing: her professional life now demanded a large amount of travel, but despite moments of loneliness when she found it hard to be away from family and friends, this was adding a great deal, too.

Indeed, travel was becoming a huge side benefit to the life she was leading now. She especially relished visiting Israel. "I went to Jerusalem, to Jesus's tomb and the place of the Last Supper," she related. "I swam in the Dead Sea. We all took our clothes off and rubbed ourselves in the boiling hot mud—very spiritual! We drove along the partition wall and saw into Palestine: it was incredible." Of course, this tapped into her Catholic background. The layers of Lady Gaga were far more complex than they may at first have seemed.

She was entering the lexicon of modern celebrity, and fast, too. Lady Gaga was beginning to have an influence and was cited as an influence on others far more often than ever before. After only a year at the top, she was starting to inhabit the same stratosphere as those who had been there for decades, whose cultural impact was tried and tested. But while many in a similar position had had their moment of glory before falling by the wayside, Gaga really did seem capable of holding on.

It was simply this: she was referenced everywhere. Far more than simply being thought of as the Next Big Thing, Lady Gaga was treated as if she'd been around for decades and was so much part of the show-business lexicon that it was entirely natural that compliments were paid to her everywhere, by everyone, just about all the time. She was mentioned constantly. After she had spent about eleven months in the spotlight, you might be forgiven for thinking that Gaga had been around for years.

There was another compliment, of sorts, when the video for "Paparazzi" was voted Creepiest Of All Time, with Chico's "Chico Time" at number two,

Michael Jackson's "Thriller" at three and David Hasselhoff's "Jump In My Car" at number four. Lady Gaga was also cited as being behind the rise in popularity of pointed bras (shades of Madonna, again), as well as perhaps owning the least wearable shoes ever made, those that featured in the video for "Bad Romance."

Designed by Alexander McQueen for his spring 2010 collection, ten-inch high "Alien" shoes were not on general sale, but there had been a massive increase in the number of women asking about them in the wake of the video. Meanwhile, Katy Perry joined the love of all things Gaga and sang a cover version of "Poker Face" (alongside a cover of Beyoncé's "Single Ladies").

That November "Video Phone," the collaboration with Beyoncé, premiered at the MTV European Music Awards in Berlin and Gaga was enthusiastic in her praise for her new friend: "You know, she is such a beautiful person, and I gotta tell you, I just adore her," she said, as she accepted the award for Best New Act. "I had kind of lost faith a little bit in meeting artists in the business and then I met Beyoncé. She is a real, real woman. I have never laughed so hard on a video set in my life. We had the best time doing 'Video Phone.'"

The video was not, however, one of the most successful projects she'd ever done. Within the industry, there was widespread feeling that Beyoncé wanted to lift some of the coolness attached to Lady Gaga onto her own image, but she did not entirely succeed. The two of them were dressed in a series of leotards and shot toy guns at men, but it was nothing like the inspired imagery of "Bad Romance" and received lukewarm reviews, with Beyoncé generally considered to have come off worst.

"So anyway, this brings me to 'Video Phone'—and what exactly is the point of Gaga featuring in this song?" asked Radio 1. "I know Beyoncé fans won't like me saying this, but I can't help but think that in this instance it's a case of 'If you can't beat 'em, join 'em.' The song is pretty average—if you're being nice about it—but it's repetitive and can come across as monotonous. If you haven't heard it, and you want to know what it sounds like, imagine someone saying over and over again, 'Watch me on your video phone, your video phone' and erm—well, that's it, really! Gaga's contribution is small and her verse lacks the originality of her solo work. Generally, the lyrics are simple, yet dripping with innuendo, backed up over a thinly-spread beat and a few orgasmic groans."

It was a rare misjudgment, though, in a career that soared higher by the day. Indeed, the makers of the TV series *Gossip Girl* were now wooing her: "I sat down with the writers and said, 'I want to do this, and the reason I want to do this is because I am trying to say something that is not mainstream in a mainstream

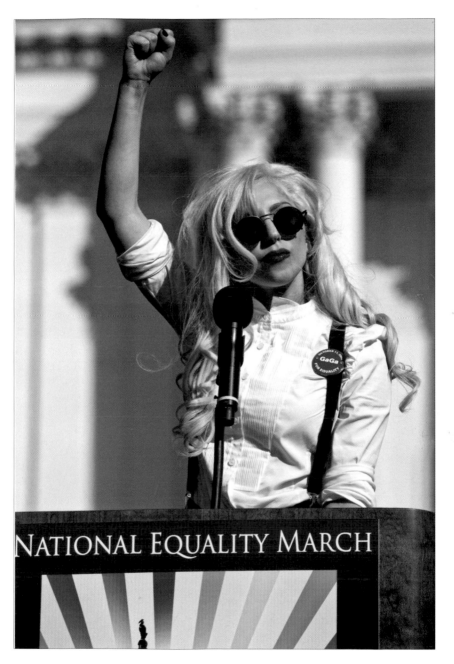

Lady Gaga is an ardent supporter of gay rights. She spoke and performed at the National Equality March on 12 October, 2009.

One of Lady Gaga's biggest fans is celebrity gossip blogger Perez Hilton. He dressed up as her – complete with hair bow – for Halloween.

Above: Lady Gaga at dinner with Lorenzo Martone and Marc Jacobs.

Below left: Arriving to receive the Stylemaker Award, which honours fashion influencers.

Below right: Gaga's tattoo is a quote from her favourite philosopher, Rainer Maria Rilke. It reads (in German): 'In the deepest hour of the night, confess to yourself that you would die if you were forbidden to write. And look deep into your heart where it spreads its roots, the answer, and ask yourself, must I write?'

Above: Lady Gaga leaving a restaurant in a completely see-through black lace dress.

Below: She appeared on 'Wetten, dass?' a German game and entertainment show and also the most successful TV show in Europe.

Above: Dr Dre and Jimmy Iovine joined Lady Gaga at her CD signing for 'The Fame Monster'.

Below left: Gaga, looking glamorous and gorgeous, with a signed copy of her CD.

Below right: Lady Gaga in her role as the creative director of Polaroid.

Lady Gaga and her father leave Cecconi's Restaurant in London.

Above: Lady Gaga performs on an elevated piano at the Royal Variety Performance 2009.

Below: Gaga's eyecatching outfit close-up (*right*) and with Miley Cyrus (*left*).

The Queen of Pop meets the Queen of England

capacity,'" said Lady Gaga. "If I can say it on your show, that would be a real coup."

Meanwhile, the enormous array of differing looks went on. One moment she was dressed as a Goth (or Frankenstein's Bride, according to one unkind observer) in New York, the next with black bra and thong visible under a sheer black top in London, and then with clown make-up, tinfoil headwear and a silver puffball dress in LA. Even the young Madonna hadn't worked this many looks and would take a couple of months to change them; in Lady Gaga's case it appeared she was trying out a new image every single day.

There was a dress with shoulder pads so wide that one newspaper remarked that it made her look like a mattress, but why should she care? Her audience adored her and she did nothing to dent that admiration when she spent over $1,000 on pizzas for fans who had waited all night long to have her sign their CD. She might have been an unlikely champion of the underdog, but given everything she had said about wanting to help those who felt like outsiders, that is what she had become. It sat comfortably alongside her work for the Gay Movement as well: another set of people who frequently had to put up with gibes for being fractionally different from everyone else.

"My relationship with the gay community has been the most incredible thing," said Lady Gaga. "I love them so much. My fans have a soul—they're a subculture of music lovers, pop music lovers, misfits . . . an incredible group of young people who all have something in common and come to my shows to be freed."

Her workload, however, continued to be horrendous. She loved it, and it was how she wanted to spend her whole time, but she was sacrificing a lot, too: "I don't go to nightclubs," she told one journalist. "If I do, I'll be one whisky and a half into it and then I have to get back to work. I love my work so much, I find it really hard to go out and have a good time. Something that I have or fear is never being able to enjoy myself."

Work was certainly her be-all and end-all at that moment, but when you want something that badly, it can be hard to slow the pace down. And she was paying a high price, too. For all the positivity she engendered, Lady Gaga had a highly melancholic streak, no doubt bred from those feelings of not fitting in when she was at school, and it could manifest itself now that she was an adult. She missed her friends, and above all, her parents, when she was touring. Indeed, sometimes it sounded as if it was all too much for her.

Asked about the low point of what had otherwise been a staggeringly good year, she replied, "Loneliness, being on the road. I have a chronic sadness that recurs. The lowest point was in Australia, in May: I was overwhelmingly sad and I didn't know why because I had all these things to be happy about. I went to the studio and played for hours, and I wrote what is going to be the greatest record of my career, a beautiful song about my father. I remember watching the mascara tears flood the ivories and I thought, 'It's OK to be sad.' I've been trained to love my darkness."

Of course, it's not unusual for artists to have their dark side, but that fact wouldn't have made it any easier for her to cope. Perhaps, given the stress she was under, the darkness was coming closer to the surface. Writing in the *Guardian*, Jude Rogers penned a brilliant analysis of what made the "Bad Romance" video so powerful and one of the elements was this hitherto un-glimpsed melancholic note. "It is the sense of sadness that gives the 'Bad Romance' video its power," he wrote. "On the surface, it is a hodgepodge of costume changes and product placements, but beyond that it makes points about the trafficking of women. But another image of her in the video is the one that lingers in the mind. This is an unvarnished Lady Gaga, wearing hardly any make-up, not dressed up or dancing, simply crying into the camera. She appears at three crucial, emotional moments: just after the trafficked version of her is forced to drink alcohol; as she sings, 'I don't want to be friends,' like a woman still in love with her ex; in the last chorus, as the song reaches its climax. It works brilliantly."

Indeed, it did, although it is to be hoped that the melancholia could be kept under control: some artists suffer quite badly if depression really manages to take hold. On the whole, Lady Gaga knew how lucky she was and how much had been given to her. She had started the year as a relative unknown and ended it as one of the most famous people on the planet. If there was a downside to it all, then that was a price she was prepared to pay. "It's been incredible," she admitted. "Truthfully, I'm just very grateful and I can't work hard enough. I've been travelling so much, I've written songs in every continent around the world, and it's been so inspiring. I love it all, and it's only made me more hungry."

And it was that attitude that would keep her up there: Gaga was only too aware that although she'd had a spectacular debut, she would need years more of this before she was really where she wanted to be. But she had the stamina and she knew what the downside was. Besides, her professional life had never been fuller.

Anyway, the rewards were so huge—who could possibly have spurned them? Certainly not Lady Gaga. She'd also had the opportunity to meet many of the people she had idolized while growing up and that, too, was just one of the many advantages to such a dedicated attitude to work and to pursuing her dream. And sometimes she still managed to sound more than a little starstruck.

"I met Grace Jones," Lady Gaga confided in one journalist. "It was a wonderful experience, she's an incredible woman, and I got to spend a little bit of time with her. It was so nice. I've been really honored by some of the people I've met, but I don't like to discuss it because it takes away the sacredness."

Indeed, she had come so far and in such a short time that the hunt was truly now on to find the new Lady Gaga. All sorts of candidates were being put forth, such as the American artist Ke$ha, but if truth be told, no one could rival the Lady herself. It was hardly any time since she'd been labelled the new Madonna and she was still at the start of her career. She wasn't about to hand over the reins to anyone just yet.

The Monster Ball Tour kicked off in Montreal, Canada on November 27, 2009—to no one's surprise, it was a complete sell-out. Gaga, however, was beginning to dream of a personal life in the future: "I want a husband and children," she said. "In eight to ten years, I want to have babies for my dad to hold, grand-kids. I want to have a husband who loves and supports me, just the way anyone else does. I would never leave my career for a man right now and I would never follow a man around."

She couldn't help sounding like the traditional Catholic girl that she still was, deep inside. Nor was that work ethic anything new, as she revealed in an interview with *Elle*, when she talked about working as a waitress when she was younger: "I got big tips," she said. "I always wore heels to work! I told everybody stories and for customers on dates, I kept it romantic. It's like performing."

In the same interview, however, she also revealed how stress could take its toll. "I get all the symptoms of a pregnant woman," she admitted. "I get headaches, I get tired and sometimes I get blurred vision." In truth, it sounded as if she was doing too much, but there was to be no let-up, not just yet.

In December, it was back to Britain, where two American giants, Lady Gaga and Janet Jackson, appeared on *The X Factor* finale. Lady Gaga sang "Bad Romance:" this time she writhed around in a giant bathtub. And there were more weird and wonderful outfits: a transparent rubber dress with fishnets and a pair of antlers were spotted on the streets.

She also performed at the O2 Capital FM Jingle Bell Ball in a red bra and panties—well, it *was* nearly Christmas. That show was also a huge success and she was about to perform in front of the British Queen. Gaga had taken the international world by storm. Could she keep it up? Definitely! Success was building on success.

CHAPTER 14

THE QUEEN
GOES GAGA

THE SCENE WAS THE SEASIDE RESORT OF Blackpool, where the Royal Variety Performance was to take place for the first time in fifty-four years. Queen Elizabeth II, eighty-three, and her eighty-eight-year-old husband, Prince Philip, were among the audience and they were about to witness one of the most extraordinary acts ever to appear since the show first began. Lady Gaga had taken up the challenge presented to her—how to outdo everything she had done before—with a relish.

And she managed it. For a start, there was the tricky question of what to wear. It is unlikely that she would have been overly concerned about displaying too much flesh in front of the Queen, but in the event she went in totally the opposite direction and covered up as never before. Indeed, she appeared to be paying homage to the Queen's antecedents, for although her dress was made of red latex, it was a long gown with a giant ruff at the neck, plus a very lengthy train. It was the kind of garment that Elizabeth I might have worn, had latex been around in the sixteenth century and the Her Majesty been a pop star. The look was finished off with matching red boots and eye-patches (with glitter on them), for that extra-special effect.

Then there was the set. Lady Gaga was to play the piano, but this was not your average grand. This one appeared to have been inspired by Salvador Dali's painting, "The Temptation of St. Anthony:" with its strange, giant elephant legs, it towered above the stage. "Good evening, Blackpool," announced Gaga. "Let me hear you rattle your jewellery!" An assistant helped her onto a swing, which then rose about thirty feet in the air so that she could reach the keyboard. She launched into "Speechless," the song she had written for her father Joe, who was in the audience to hear his little girl sing. Her train hung down to the ground; a small orchestra to accompany her performance nestled at the foot of the giant piano.

Afterwards, she was presented to the Queen and executed a deep curtsy: Her Majesty beamed in return. Indeed, there were some reports that she was so amused by Lady Gaga's performance that she ordered aides to Google her, although this was never officially confirmed.

It was a spectacular performance and one that

would surely not have been possible had Gaga been a sufferer of vertigo, but it was a toned-down act for the performer herself. "I wanted to do the suicide scene but was told it wouldn't be appropriate," she revealed. "I've also had to tone things down generally, but it doesn't matter because I'm a massive fan of the Queen—I was so excited and have even been practising my curtsy."

And she certainly seemed to be enjoying her UK stay. She was pictured in various pubs, in the usual bizarre get-ups, and eating fish and chips. There were no airs or graces about her: on the contrary, she often appeared thoroughly dignified. But she was only in town briefly before hopping back across the Atlantic to get up to her old tricks, telling the American broadcast journalist Barbara Walters, "I have had sexual relations with women, but I've only ever been in love with men. . . ." Everyone had got the gist of it now: she was a wild woman and one not easy to categorize.

She had something else to say to Walters, too—it simply wasn't the case that she was out to shock. When asked about the biggest misconception surrounding her, she said: "That I am artificial and attention-seeking, when the truth is every bit of me is devoted to love and art. I aspire to be a teacher to my young fans, who feel just like I felt when I was younger. I want to free them of their fears and make them feel they can create their own place in the world."

This was a theme that came up, time and again.

It must be said, however, that it wasn't always clear what she was talking about. "If you're on an island and all you have is sticks, leaves and pineapples, you're gonna make a boat out of sticks, leaves and pineapples," she told one audience while performing in Vancouver. "I spend my career harvesting pineapples, making pies and outfits that'll free my fans." Still, it didn't matter—she remained the most wildly entertaining star around. She also upset the local authorities by lighting a cigarette onstage (smoking indoors is illegal in British Columbia), this time wearing a minuscule gold two-piece teamed with fishnets. The recent reticence inspired by the Queen was clearly no more.

Although she had no shortage of detractors, it was noticeable that her admirers included some of the greatest performers of the day. Sir Elton John had been no slouch when it came to outrageous performances and garments himself, and his partner David Furnish was enthusiastic in his praise. "Lady Gaga is fabulous," he declared. "She's amazing! I love how she's created this persona with a completely individual sense of style. I like people like her in music.

"It's like Boy George in the Culture Club days— he was an original. During the seventies, eighties and nineties, David Bowie and Elton pushed the boundaries and barriers of what fashion as a performer means;

Madonna, too. They make the world a much more colorful and happy place—it keeps life interesting."

It being December, round-ups of albums of the year began, and *The Fame* featured in many of those. Neil McCormick of the *Daily Telegraph* was a typical example of what the critics felt: "But arguably the two artists whose albums have come closest to defining 2009 are bold women, Lily Allen with her witty, outspoken *It's Not Me, It's You*, and Lady Gaga, with her electro, self-conscious, über-pop escapism *The Fame*," he wrote. "These are albums that have personality, color and big, memorable pop songs, managing to hit commercial highs without sacrificing intelligence or artistry."

The *Independent On Sunday* had her as its Face of the Year: "The face of pop in 2009 belonged to Stefani Germanotta, a twenty-three-year-old New Yorker, although actually seeing that face was never easy behind the feathers, warpaint and masks," it observed. "Already a transatlantic star by the end of 2008 with two British No 1s to her name, Lady Gaga touched down in the UK in the summer with a live show that proved her to be not just the junior Madonna we'd imagined, but also something approaching a young, female Prince: flamboyant, prodigiously talented, sexually predatory and entirely self-created."

As the year drew to an end, Gaga triumphs racked up. When informed that she'd sold eight million albums, she broke down in tears onstage while continuing to prove herself adept as ever at generating publicity. She did a nude photo shoot with Kanye West, recreating some of cinema's greatest *film noir* moments (in one shot, her modesty is protected by strategically placed tabloid headlines). Onstage in Atlanta, Georgia, she even managed to react with aplomb when someone threw a bunch of flowers at her head: she merely straightened her hat and carried on.

She reacted rather more strongly, however, during a night out in Ottawa, Canada. Lady Gaga and her friends were enjoying themselves when a fellow clubber began to make himself obnoxious, telling her that she and her friend Adam Lambert, the openly gay star of *American Idol*, were freaks and would go to hell: "OK, that's it," said Gaga, pouring a glass of wine over his head. "Call me anything you want, but when you start calling my friends names, it's war!" With that, she walked out.

Of course, there had been one other female success story that year—Susan Boyle. Susan, a shy Scottish spinster of a certain age, could hardly have been more different to the flamboyant diva, but the Lady herself was of the opinion that perhaps they might do something together in the future: after all, why not? Both had suddenly risen out of nowhere and set the world ablaze.

"I love Susan Boyle, she is my Woman of the

Year—I don't know if we could work together, but never say never," she said. "Our styles are different. It would be great to work with somebody of that talent. She has achieved more in this year than most artists will in a lifetime. This time last year nobody even knew who she was and now she is knocking the world's most established artists off the album and singles charts."

Funnily enough, various other creative minds had been musing on the same subject. *Vogue* put together a stunning *mise-en-scene* based on the fairy tale of Hansel and Gretel, photographed by celebrity snapper Annie Leibovitz and styled by the magazine's creative director Grace Coddington: Hansel and Gretel were played by Andrew Garfield and Lily Cole, while Coddington originally wanted Susan for the role of the Wicked Witch. The decision was eventually vetoed by editor Anna Wintour and the part went to none other than Lady Gaga, who ended up looking wonderfully wild and ethereal.

With Gaga's popularity showing no sign of waning, ever more ingenious ways were being introduced to sell the records. She herself now offered fans the chance to own a lock of her hair: if they bought the Gaga Super-Deluxe Fame Monster Bundle, not only would they get said hair, but a puzzle, posters, a paper doll collection and a personal note from the performer, too—all for about $110.

In January 2010, Polaroid picked her as its new

chief creative director—"I am so excited to extend myself behind the scenes as a designer and to, as my father puts it, finally have a real job," said Gaga. Indeed, for someone as image-obsessed as her, the appointment had certain symmetry. Nor was she planning on being just a figurehead: "I'm so proud to announce my partnership with Polaroid," she continued. "The Haus of Gaga has been developing prototypes in the fields of fashion and technology."

The ability to create extraordinary images remained. Shortly after the Polaroid link-up was announced, she appeared with her own hair teased into the shape of a giant sun hat. She then made various appearances on the balcony of the hotel where she was staying: first, almost naked except for a towel and then in an ostentatious display of underwear. But it kept up the public interest, so why not?

She also refused to let up the pace, determined to release her third album by the end of 2010: "That's the beauty of writing your own music—you don't have to rely on songwriters and producers to come up with hit songs for you," she declared. "I wrote *The Fame Monster* during the last tour, so I assume that it will inspire some kind of new sonic energy and lyrical style."

Meanwhile, the outfits continued to amaze. At the beginning of the New Year, Lady Gaga was seen having dinner at Nobu in Miami with Perez Hilton: her hair was yellow, rather than its usual blonde; she wore a gray rubber skirt and black PVC jacket (which looked as if it had been shredded), fishnets, black PVC boots, a black hat and sunglasses. Perez gave as good as he got: his ensemble was made up of a T-shirt featuring Madonna, a black silk jacket, banana-covered boxers, gold running shoes—and sunglasses.

But perhaps the ultimate and most fitting accolade came in early January 2010, when it was announced that Lady Gaga was to become a character in a comic book. A new series of celebrity comics were being launched by Bluewater Productions and titled, appropriately enough, *Fame*. Gaga was to be its first-ever star—others down the line would include Robert Pattinson, Taylor Swift, David Beckham and the American rapper, 50 Cent. Inevitably, there was much joking about the fact that she already resembled a comic-book character, but this, more than anything else, showed quite how far she had come. It was official: Lady Gaga was a phenomenon. And she had only just begun.

THE WORLD
ACCORDING TO
LADY GAGA

NE OF THE MOST REMARKABLE FACETS OF the rise and rise of Lady Gaga is quite how quickly she became part of the national scenery. One moment no one had heard of her and the next it was as if she'd been around for years. There were many reasons for this, not least her talent and originality, but one in particular is that she somehow managed to combine all society's obsessions into one. Fame, talent, celebrity, our society cannot get enough of them, and when a highly intelligent pop star makes those obsessions her chosen subject, it's not hard to see why the world fell in love.

For that is essentially what happened. For all her chat about loving men and sleeping with women, the most important relationship for Lady Gaga outside her family is with her fans. She has frequently spoken about being an outsider at school: now, she isn't anymore. By being true to herself, she's become one of the world's leading stars in her field, but she has paid the price. Solitude, she has revealed, is "something you marry, as an artist. When you are an artist, your solitude is a lonely place that you embrace."

She certainly isn't your average pop star either. On tour in Japan, she revealed her most recent tattoo: a quote (in German) from Rainer Maria Rilke, whom she described as her favorite philosopher—the "philosopher of solitude." That quote is another way of showing her dedication to her art: "It says: 'In the deepest hour of the night, confess to yourself that you would die if you were forbidden to write. And look deep into your heart where it spreads its roots, the answer, and ask yourself, must I write?'" she revealed. It is safe to say that Britney Spears is unlikely to have a similar piece of body art.

No one since Madonna has been more aware of the power of appearance and so, despite numerous forays into different looks, at heart remains the long blonde hair, sometimes tied into a bow. "And I guess that somehow became my signature look," she told one journalist. "But more importantly, I believe in the power of iconography, which was something that Andy Warhol did, and it's repeating an image over and over again, so I rarely change the shape of my hair."

Then there was the slightly unexpected vulnerability. On the one hand, this was a woman who could take to the stage in her panties and a firing bra: you wouldn't necessarily call her a blushing violet. And so media-savvy was Lady Gaga that she had actually managed to make a star out of her own teacup. But there was a totally different side to her, as well: Gaga, that living, breathing embodiment of avant-garde art, was also a nice girl who loved her parents and couldn't live without their approval. It was her father's disapproval that stopped her from becoming a full-on druggie. Without his love and support, she quite openly admitted that she wouldn't be able to cope. Groundbreaking artiste she might be, but she'd be nothing without her dad.

Then there was that love affair with the drummer, which she has not to this day opened up about, and which clearly hurt her. In this, she was unlike Madonna, who has never displayed vulnerability about anything, but it made Lady Gaga all the more appealing and helped her audiences to relate to her. In rising above it, she has become a strong woman: she might have been knocked about by life, but ultimately, she can deal with it all.

Gaga has also created a quiet reference library for her fans: motifs that appear and reappear throughout her work, some quirky and personal, some they can recognize and claim as their own. The first of these was in fact someone else's: the lightning make-up strike that adorned David Bowie on the cover of *Aladdin Sane*. Lady Gaga took it and made it her own, so much so that her father even acquired his own tattoo in honour of his massively talented daughter. And while Bowie's was multi-colored, Lady Gaga's comes in all sorts of permutations, including black.

Then there were all sorts of other references, too. Teacups, obviously, figured largely. So, less obviously, did Great Danes. Lady Gaga featured a pair of Great Danes, Lava and her son Rumpus, over and over in her videos, including "Poker Face," "Love Game" and "Paparazzi," before poor Rumpus unexpectedly died just before the "Bad Romance" video, leaving his mother to carry on (which she did—she is in the first shot). And then came the exploding bras: she managed a coup there. Not even the mighty Madonna had latched onto that.

Lady Gaga is often teased for taking herself so seriously, but why not? Joanne Stefani Germanotta has done what few have been able to do: she has taken an image, an established persona, and turned herself into it. In many ways, she is the ultimate pop star. Many people seek fame because of the rewards it will bring: the riches, the acclaim, the mansions, plus the cars and the lovers. Lady Gaga is not like that at all.

She cares about what she does because it has an intrinsic value. Her work is totally slick, polished and professional. It has struck a chord with countries across the world, tired of manufactured pop icons, who want to see the real deal: Lady Gaga *is* the real deal. It is almost painful to see how much she cares about her work—she puts body and soul into it. Her life is her own creation, and incredibly impressive for all that.

When she played the Royal Variety Performance, she was very covered up by her standards, yet outrageous at the same time. In the aftermath, there was a good deal of joking that the Queen herself could not have been taken aback because she'd seen it all before. But that was not, in fact, entirely true: she'd never witnessed the likes of Gaga before, but then neither had anyone else. She was that most unusual of Noughties' beings—a real one of a kind.

And finally, there's her extraordinary talent. Many pop stars can sing and dance, but few can play an instrument and almost none of them compose their own material. Lady Gaga can do all those things, and more. The world of pop hasn't seen anything like her since the young Madonna—and even Madonna doesn't have all the talents that Lady Gaga has so far displayed. The future is going to be massive.

DISCOGRAPHY

The Fame, Interscope Records, August 19, 2008.

The Fame Monster, Interscope Records, November 23, 2009.